Little Dogs:

TRAINING your **Pint-Sized** companion

Deborah Wood

TRAINING your Pint-Sized companion

T.F.H. Publications, Inc.

Front cover photo courtesy of Creatas.
Back cover photo by Carole Archer.
Author photo by Lamm Photography, Inc.
Book design by Cándida M. Tómassini.

T.F.H. Publications
President/CEO: Glen S. Axelrod
Executive Vice President: Mark E. Johnson
Publisher: Christopher T. Reggio
Production Manager: Kathy Bontz

T.F.H. Publications, Inc.
One TFH Plaza
Third and Union Avenues
Neptune City, NJ 07753

Printed and Bound in China
07 08 09 10 11   3 5 7 9 8 6 4

ISBN13 978-0-7938-0537-2

Library of Congress Cataloging-in-Publication Data
Wood, Deborah, 1952-
     Little dogs : training your pint-sized companion / Deborah Wood.
                    p. cm.
                    Includes bibliographical references.
          ISBN 0-7938-0537-6 (alk. paper)
          1.   Dogs-Training. I. Title.
     SF431.W678 2004
     636.7'0887–dc22
     2003022762

This book has been published with the intent to provide accurate and authoritative information in regard to the subject matter within. While every reasonable precaution has been taken in preparation of this book, the author and publisher expressly disclaim responsibility for any errors, omissions, or adverse effects arising from the use or application of the information contained herein. The techniques and suggestions are used at the reader's discretion and are not to be considered a substitute for veterinary care. If you suspect a medical problem consult your veterinarian.

The Leader In Responsible Animal Care For Over 50 Years!®
www.tfh.com

Table of Contents

CHAPTER 10
Cool Stuff to Do With Your Trained Dog 107

CHAPTER 11
Advanced Obedience Training 121

CHAPTER 12
Reflections on Life With Small Dogs 129

Resources 133

Index 139

English Toy Spaniels

The Wonderful (and Challenging) World of Small Dogs

*F*orget about running with the wolves. In many ways, small dogs teach us more about the mystery and magic of canines than their larger cousins can. There is no more intimate experience in dogdom than sharing your life with a small dog. This little guy undoubtedly follows you from room to room; he probably even follows you into the bathroom, just to keep tabs on your activities.

He hops on your lap when you're reading or watching TV. You routinely take him with you on every errand, and he may even come to work with you. If you're retired, this pooch is with you 24 hours a day. Even if your previous dogs slept on the floor, chances are that your small dog sleeps in bed with you.

The Joys of Small Dogs

There's a pocket-sized pooch for every kind of dog-lover: scrappy, teeny terriers; energetic Papillons who love to herd, jump, and run; patient Shih Tzu and Japanese Chin who like nothing better than to share the TV with you; stalwart Pomeranians; cheeky Miniature Pinschers—every small breed (and mix) has its own delights.

Though small in stature, little dogs have tremendous hearts and an abundance of love and affection to share.

These dogs can do everything their larger cousins can do, but they do it in less space, and the humans in the household don't have to be toned athletes to keep the dogs in shape. Your small dog has a spirit that's every bit as big as animals that are ten times his size. He just comes in a handier package.

Small dogs fit into our lives in a way big dogs just can't. Living so closely with each other, we breathe the same air, we experience the same places, we feel each other's heartbeats. Your connection with your small dog may be the most profound bond you'll have with an animal in your lifetime.

The popularity of lap-sized dogs is growing exponentially. In fact, 12 of the AKC's 20 most popular breeds of 2002 typically weigh 15 pounds or less. While registrations of most breeds have dropped over the last few years, registration of almost every toy and small breed has risen, and sometimes their numbers have doubled in the space of just a few years.

The Challenges of Small Dogs

While it can be incredibly rewarding to share your life with a small dog, it can also be just plain frustrating. The toy breeds are notoriously hard to housetrain. When they decide not to come when called, you have a pocket-sized rocket careening around—even racing between your feet—that you can't grab. Then there's the barking, barking, barking, barking, and more barking that quickly becomes the habit of many little dogs. And having a tiny terror that snaps and growls at everyone within 10 feet of you really isn't funny.

Traditional training methods don't work well with little dogs. You may have had the stomach-wrenching experience of giving your dog the same kind of tug on the leash that you used to give to your Labrador, just to see your poor little pooch fly through the air. Or you've tried to teach your Dachshund to lie down by putting a treat on the floor, only to realize that even standing on his tiptoes, your dog's nose is already on the floor. The advice to push lightly on a dog's rump to teach him to sit can injure your toy breed puppy. This book will give you practical methods that work for your small dog and are fun and positive for you both.

Why Training Matters

Lots of people will tell you that training your small dog is optional. Really, how much trouble can a little ball of fluff get into? The answer, sadly, is a lot.

If your small dog doesn't come when he's called, he's in special danger. Let's face it: It's harder for the driver of a car to see your 5-pound Maltese than the neighbor's 150-pound Mastiff. Coming when called can't be an option, but way too few people train this simple command to their little dogs.

Then there are the armpit piranhas: little dogs who bare their teeth and growl at everyone who comes within 10 feet of their humans. That seems pretty funny until you realize that the odds are that your dog is frightened and needs to turn to you for leadership. This dog will certainly be happier and may even live longer if you teach him some basic boundaries.

Just as important, training your small dog is just plain fun. Your little dog has all the brains and the instincts of dogs that outweigh him by 100 pounds. Too many little dogs live lives of constant boredom. Not only do these dogs sometimes get themselves into big trouble (humans almost never like it when dogs make their own fun), but they're missing out on the profound, magical bond that comes from sharing positive obedience training together.

You already love your dog, and he loves you. But, after you follow the training suggestions in this book, you'll find yourself more bonded and attached than you could have ever imagined before. This kind of training will open doors of communication and joy between you and your dog that you've probably never experienced before.

This book is designed with the small dog in mind. It will take you, step-by-step, through techniques that will work for your small-breed dog or puppy. Every technique is positive, leaving your dog wagging his tail and you smiling with pride at your clever little friend.

Putting Yourself in Your Dog's Paws

Because our dogs have all the intelligence and instincts of their larger cousins, sometimes we forget that they're little. But the fact is that it's not the same to be a 3-pound dog, or even a 15- or 20-pound dog, as it is to be a sturdy 80-pound or 150-pound giant breed. Just think: There's the same difference between an 8-pound dog and an 80-pound dog as there is between a 150-pound person and a 1,500-pound horse!

Lie down on the floor and put your eyes at your dog's level. From your little dog's perspective, you seem as tall as a four-story building seems to a human. Imagine how scary it is to your little one if that huge creature starts yelling.

People often say, "My dog thinks he's a big dog." Nothing could be further from the truth. Your dog may have all the courage of a big dog and certainly has all the brains. What he knows he doesn't have is a big dog's size, and he's right. When he's growling and snapping at the big dogs, it's because he figures that he's safer being an aggressor.

Look at the size of your dog's legs—they may be more slender than your finger, and think of his fine spine and delicate hips. Your little dog needs to feel safe. Gentle, non-forced, happy training methods will give your dog that sense of safety and confidence.

While positive training methods are good for all dogs, they're essential for small ones. Fortunately, today we know we don't have to yell, jerk, hit, or pull to make a dog learn. In fact, dogs learn faster when they're given rewards (including food, toys, attention, and praise) for doing things right. And, because force just isn't an option for a creature that may be one-twentieth your size, you'll find that this dog will probably learn faster and have more fun than any other dog you've ever owned.

FEAR VERSUS MOTIVATION

I start every small dog obedience course I teach with a demonstration that shows just how much more effective positive methods are than negative ones. I pick out a (hopefully!) good sport from the class and ask that person to be my "demo dog." I ask the "demo dog" to sit on a bench in the training facility.

Because small dogs have little bodies, gentle, positive training methods will help them feel safe.

"Stand up!" I scream. The startled person usually stands pretty quickly.

"Sit down!" I yell. The person sits.

"Stand again!" I screech at the top of my lungs. The demo dog stands more slowly.

"Sit down!"

"Stand up!"

After I repeat the commands a couple of times, you can see the person getting visibly angry. Some stop moving; others glare at me and respond slowly.

Then I ask for another "demo dog" from the group.

"Will you please sit over here?" I ask in a friendly voice. When the person does, I smile and give the demo dog a quarter. "That was excellent!" I exclaim.

"Will you please stand?" I ask again in a soft, happy way. The person stands and gets a dime. "That was great!"

"And can you sit again?" Another quarter.

"Would you mind standing?" Then I clap my hands and tell everyone to cheer for the great way the demo dog is standing. The person is always smiling and is happy and eager to try anything I ask, even though she knows it's just a silly game.

I always ask the two demo dogs to describe their experiences. The first one uses words like "frustrated" and "angry" to explain what it was like to be my imaginary dog. The second demo dog always uses words like "fun" and usually asks to do more!

The same is true for your dog. If you are always yelling and demanding more and more of the dog without (in doggie language!) telling him you're happy, he'll get frustrated and upset. If you encourage him and tell him that he's great, he'll try to do even better the next time. Humans and dogs have a lot in common that way!

THE DOG GAME: GAINING A NEW PERSPECTIVE

It's unbelievably hard to be a dog in our human world. We expect so much of all dogs and even more of our small dogs. They're supposed to understand our commands, be in tune with our moods, and live in our cities. And when they aren't perfect, we often label them as stupid or stubborn.

Once you play the Dog Game (sometimes called the Training Game) you'll gain a whole new insight into just how much we ask of our dogs. It just takes two to play this game: a "Dog" and a "Trainer." The Trainer picks a behavior she wants the dog to do. This should not be a typical dog command, such as sit, come, or speak. After all, the "Dog" already knows what we expect real dogs to learn. We want the Dog to experience what it's like to learn something new, from a real dog's perspective.

The Trainer should think of a single action. Example of behaviors include having the Dog touch her hand to her face, walk to a wall and touch it, hop on one foot, or walk in a counter-clockwise circle.

Once a behavior is decided upon, the Trainer can't give any verbal clues. (After all, real dogs don't understand English!) The Trainer can just say, "Good!" to the Dog when she does something that approximates the desired behavior. So, if you want the Dog to touch her face with her hand, say, "Good!" every time the Dog moves her hand. When she moves her hand upwards, get very happy and excited.

This seems like a simple exercise, but it can revolutionize your view of dog training. If you are the Dog, you quickly understand just how hard and frustrating it is to figure out what the Trainer is trying to get you to do. It will give you a whole new respect for what dogs figure out from us!

If you are the Trainer, you'll realize that you're getting through to a dog much less than you thought. Dogs are so good at trying to figure out what we want that we don't realize how hard we are to understand, until a human tells us point-blank that we were very confusing.

Recognizing your dog's perspective is the first step in forging a solid training relationship with him.

Take the time to grab a human friend and play the Dog Game. Reading about it is one thing—doing it is a thousand times more dramatic. As you train your real dog, think about the lessons of the Dog Game. Don't be too quick to assume your dog is lazy, stupid, or stubborn. More likely than not, he just can't figure out what you're asking him to do. Figure out what you need to do differently to teach him, not what he needs to do differently to learn.

When we train from the dog's perspective, our dogs will learn faster and better than when we only think of ourselves. At least as important, we will strengthen and develop a bond of mutual respect and trust that will last a lifetime—the ultimate reward.

Miniature Dachshund

Special Issues for Small Dogs

chapter 2

Safely Training a Small Breed

Dogs, especially our small companion breeds, are genetically programmed to live in harmony with humans. They have an incredible ability to adapt to our lifestyles and even learn what much of our language means. It's easy to forget that each puppy needs to learn for himself just how to be a part of a human family. Every individual—human or dog—needs to relearn the lessons of the species. For example, children are genetically wired to be able to speak and read language, but they must be taught to do so. Similarly, our small dogs have an unparalleled innate ability to bond with humans and enjoy our world, but they can't fully do so until we teach them how.

Your puppy's future is in your hands. As hard as this responsibility is with any animal, in some ways it's harder with a small-breed puppy. He probably fits in the palm of your hand. He's breakable and vulnerable, but he also seriously needs certain kinds of exposure to help him turn into a happy, confident, adaptable dog. Here are some steps you should take during the first year of his life.

UNTIL THREE MONTHS OF AGE

For small-breed puppies, the first three months of life are best spent with mom at the breeder's home. Small puppies don't have the body weight to be resilient to disease and temperature changes. They often experience hypoglycemia and have blood sugar levels that can fluctuate and need the supervision of an expert eye. This said: Don't take a small breed puppy home until he is at least 12 weeks old!

If you do have a puppy who is younger than 12 weeks old, spend the intervening time letting him explore the small world of your home. Make sure he meets some gentle children at your house. (Borrow some neighborhood kids if you don't have any of your own.) Expose him to different surfaces, such as carpeting, linoleum, and grass. He can go on some car rides, and of course, go to the veterinarian's for checkups and his shots. Still, under 12 weeks of age in the life of a small-breed puppy isn't the time to take him out much into the world: It's the time for him to learn that his home environment is interesting, safe, and fun and that people of all ages are kind and gentle.

TWELVE WEEKS TO SIX MONTHS

Forget the old adage about one human year equaling seven dog years. Instead, for the first two years of your dog's life, think of one year equaling one month. At ages three to six months, your puppy is the canine equivalent of a preschooler. This is the time to introduce him to the world, under your gentle guidance and protection. The lessons he learns during these months will form his view of the world throughout his lifetime. Are people something scary or wonderful? Are other dogs mean or potential playmates?

Any dog's ticket to fun is being reliable on a collar and leash. Find (or make) a tiny collar that fits your small pup. Make sure your puppy's collar is on snugly enough that he can't wiggle out of it. A loose collar is a real danger to an inquisitive puppy; you don't want him getting it caught on something and potentially strangling. (For indoor use only you might consider a break-away cat collar, because it

teaching a puppy his name

Most people hate their names. If we have a common name (like Deborah), we wish we'd been named Evangeline or Phoebe. I have a friend with the cool name of Markie, who always fantasized about being named Karen. If you introduce your puppy to his name the right way, I promise that he'll love his name throughout his life.

Remember, he has no idea what his name is until you teach it to him. Say his name and give him a tiny puppy treat. Repeat a few times and you'll have a puppy who loves the sound of his name. As soon as he begins to recognize his name, only use the food reward occasionally, but always reward him when he looks at you.

So, sometimes when you say, "Spot!" and he looks at you, give him a puppy treat. Other times, say, "Spot" and reward him with a tummy rub or with a "Good boy!" Make it fun for him to look at you.

Remember that Spot is just his name. When someone says, "Deborah," I merely look over and acknowledge the person who is calling to me. He doesn't expect me to come, sit, or stay, just look. When you say, "Spot," you are just asking for your puppy's attention. Then you can ask him to come, sit, or whatever command is appropriate for the occasion.

allows the puppy to wriggle free if he's snagged on something. A cat collar is a very unwise choice outside, since that same break-away feature can allow him to get loose in the dangerous outside world.)

Let your puppy wear his collar for a week or so without trying to put on a leash. It's got to feel strange and uncomfortable for a puppy to have this cord encircling his neck. After a few days, snap a very lightweight leash on. Hold on to the leash and follow the puppy everywhere he leads you. Don't try to direct him at first—you don't want the leash to be scary or intimidating, just a pleasant way of exploring the world together. If your puppy is worried, talk happily with him. (Not baby-talk! Don't say, "Oh my poor little baby, please don't be scared!" Instead say, "You are so handsome in your pretty leash! You're acting like a big guy now!")

After a few days of letting your puppy lead you, then you can begin leading your puppy. Pat your knee and in a high-pitched, happy voice, say his name and then say, "Let's go!" Take a few steps, encouraging him to follow. When he does, tell him he's the best puppy on earth.

During the first couple of weeks, alternate letting the puppy take you places and taking the puppy places. Now that your puppy is safe and secure in a collar, you can start exploring the larger world together. It's the beginning of a lifetime of teamwork.

All of this rapport and basic training are appropriate for your puppy from age three months forward. These gentle techniques are fun for dogs of any age. Just remember that puppies, like toddlers, don't have long attention spans, so just work with your pup a

Any dog's ticket to fun is being reliable on a collar and leash.

few minutes at a time and don't expect him to have behaviors requiring patience, such as "stays," longer than a few seconds at a time until he's six months or older. A foundation of basic training and leadership from you will give your pup a fabulous head start in life.

FROM SIX TO TWELVE MONTHS

Every parent watches with a certain fascinated horror as her adorable, sweet six-year-old morphs into a sassy pre-adolescent and then a surly teen. While the change isn't so dramatic in our dogs, it's still there. It's normal for the next generation of every species to figure out its place in the world. Will you be a leader? A follower? The "teen" puppy months are the time your little dog makes those decisions.

Your sweet puppy who always came to you in a heartbeat may suddenly decide that the come command is an elective course. And why should he listen when you tell him to stop chasing the cat; after all, who elected you pack leader? He certainly didn't!

While the leadership exercises in this book are important throughout your dog's life, they are especially important during those sometimes terrible teens. Your pup needs to be reminded in a gentle, safe, loving way that you are, in fact, the lead dog. You've always been the lead dog. You're always going to be the lead dog. He can relax and enjoy being part of such an excellent pack.

those sharp puppy teeth

It's natural for puppies to explore things with their mouths and their sharp little teeth. If you say, "Ouch!" and stop playing with your puppy the moment he bites down too hard, most puppies will quickly get the idea and won't use you as their favorite chew toy. Sometimes just saying "Ouch!" isn't enough. Puppies who didn't have littermates, who were taken from their, mothers too early, or are just naturally pushy sometimes don't pick up on your subtle hints.

If the puppy is persistent, even after you have repeatedly said "Ouch!" and stopped playing with the puppy every time he bites too hard, try making biting you a slightly unpleasant experience. At the back of your puppy's mouth, there is a space on his gums where there aren't any teeth. When this very persistent puppy bites your finger, gently put your fingers on his gums on that spot. Don't gag your dog, don't struggle, don't put your finger down his throat—just leave your finger for a moment or two in that gap behind his teeth. This is mildly unpleasant for your dog. If you do that every time he tries to bite you, soon he'll give up, because it's no longer fun.

Remember: Don't ever hit or yell at your dog if he bites you. It will make the problem worse, and you will have to deal with an aggressive dog for a long time to come.

While constant questioning of your authority is usually resolved after about a year, every once in a while it may come up again. At ages two and three, some dogs make one last try to take over. If you introduce a new dog—or even a cat or bird—to the house, your dog may decide it's time to see just how high up the social ladder he can go. Consistently keep up with his training and practice the leadership routines, and your household will settle back down. I promise!

Just as some humans are ambitious and work hard to get to the top, while others are content with being part of the gang, some dogs are more ambitious than others. Don't worry if you have a pushy dog, and don't be concerned if you have one who only wants to please you. One of the joys of living with dogs is the wonderful array of their personalities. Each animal relates to us and to each other in his own unique way.

SOCIALIZATION

Your dog's most important job during puppyhood is to learn to be at ease with humans and other dogs. Socialization should be the number-one priority for you and your puppy.

Your small dog lives in a world of large humans. It's important for him to meet people of all ages, shapes, sizes, and colors during this important time.

Unfortunately, the critical time for socialization happens at the identical time that your puppy is receiving his immunization shots for such deadly diseases as distemper and parvovirus. Until he's fully immunized (at about four months), your puppy can pick up some viruses when he romps through grass that's been contaminated by a sick dog.

You need to balance your little guy's absolute need for socialization with his critical need for safety. Make smart choices about where you expose your puppy. Avoid public parks, rest stops, and other places where you'll find dogs with unknown health and vaccination histories. On the other hand, it's a good idea to take your puppy to friends' homes who don't have dogs, or whose gentle dogs receive excellent veterinary care.

Just as human beings are possessed of different personalities, so too are dogs.

Make all interactions happy. If a puppy meets new people and new dogs and has a bad time, all he's learning is that people and other dogs are scary. It's the good experiences that make a dog social. Expose your pup to children, but nice ones. Don't make your puppy endure a child who is grabbing at his fur, running around, or screeching. Look for a quiet, polite child who will gently pet your little pal and give him a treat, or maybe play a little game of fetch.

Expose your puppy to a huge variety of people and experiences, including everything from umbrellas to people on skateboards, power tools, the beach, and cats. Carry treats with you and give the puppy praise and a tidbit when he explores the world. This teaches him that new experiences are a fun part of the life of a dog.

Watch for signs of stress in your puppy: a tail tucked under the rump, ears down, head down, or yawning. If you see stress, back off and slow down. Gradually work up to your little dog accepting the new experience.

MAKING FRIENDS WITH OTHER DOGS

Dogs need socialization with other dogs, and small-breed dogs are no exception. Generally, the more experienced your pint-sized pooch is with social interaction, the less likely he is to be attacked by another dog, because he'll be accustomed to giving and receiving appropriate body language.

Seek out other small dogs for your puppy to play with. All over the country, people are setting up play days for their small-breed dogs. There are Pug,

Chihuahua, Boston Terrier, and Papillon play days in many major cities. If there's not a group in your area, consider starting one for your breed or for small-sized dogs in general.

Under no circumstances should you let your small dog play with a dog that is substantially bigger than he is. Don't rely on someone else's assurance that his or her big dog won't hurt yours. Even a friendly, sweet dog can break your dog's delicate bones in play. It isn't worth the risk.

radar's scary day

I know from first-hand experience just how scary a bad interaction with a big dog can be. I was on a walk with Radar and Goldie when I felt a big dog staring at my little ones. Then he came at us, his body stretched out in a dead run. He wasn't fighting and he wasn't playing; he was hunting, and my 7-pound dogs were the game.

My dogs have an emergency "lift up" command, so before the Labrador-mix could get to us, my dogs were in my arms. For the next several minutes, the dog jumped up in the air, trying to grab Radar from my hands. The dog's owner found the whole event hilarious. Six years later, Radar still has emotional scars. He worries every time I pick him up, and —despite hours of obedience practice with big, gentle, trained dogs—Radar is still scared when another dog comes too close. My dogs were lucky—at least they weren't hurt.

Despite the worries, it's ideal for your dog to get to know some reliable, gentle, well-behaved big dogs and learn to be relaxed and comfortable around them. My scary episode with Radar and the hunting dog happened before Pogo was born and came into our lives. Pogo had an experience just as profound, and that left just as lasting an impression. Pogo's experience, however, was a very happy one.

When Pogo was a young pup, he was very confident, even cocky. At the age of five months, he was occasionally barking at big dogs, something I didn't like at all. I was worried that in his youthful exuberance, Pogo would say the wrong thing to the wrong dog.

I was at a fun match (a practice dog show) with Pogo and saw some acquaintances of mine. The wife breeds show-quality Pomeranians, and the husband has a Mastiff named Sarge. This enormous dog is a champion for his looks and has an advanced obedience title, plus he lives with a houseful of Pomeranians. Sarge was the perfect big dog for Pogo to meet, up close and personal.

My friends had Sarge lie down. Seeing the two dogs nose to nose was an amazing sight. Pogo weighed in at about 6 pounds at the time; Sarge was closer to 200. Pogo had paws the size of nickels; Sarge's were the size of dinner plates. Pogo's nose was the size of a lemon drop; Sarge's nose was the size of a lemon.

Pogo swaggered up to Sarge and confidently placed his little paws on Sarge's enormous muzzle. He sniffed and wagged his tail happily as he greeted the big dog. Suddenly, Pogo's eyes grew wide, like saucers. It was as if he suddenly realized that this big hulk he was sniffing was just the dog's head! Pogo stayed in his position a bit longer, showing that he was a confident boy. Then he slowly backed off the big head. The rest of the day, he'd look over at Sarge and gently wag his tail, as if to say, "Hey! That big guy over there; he's my buddy!"

Early socialization of your small dog is crucial to his future adjustment into family life.

My puppy learned an important lesson that day. He figured out there are dogs that are bigger and stronger than he is. He never again barked at a strange, large dog. Happily, Pogo learned his place in the world from a gentle, sweet, trained dog who would never hurt him.

As an adult, Pogo gets along fabulously with dogs of all shapes and sizes. In his animal-assisted therapy work, we've even trained him to ride in carts that are pulled by huge Newfoundlands and a Bouvier des Flandres. Pogo happily rides with the kids, while his large-sized buddies take them on rides at locations like cancer camp or muscular dystrophy camp. Pogo is confident and relaxed with dogs nearly 20 times his size.

(Although Pogo is friends with these dogs, that friendship never goes beyond a touch of noses and companionable hanging-out together. Pogo and the big dogs never, ever wrestle, play, and romp. Those are great dogs, but they are too big for my 10-pound Pogo to run with.)

Some of Pogo's sane, safe, comfortable attitude around big dogs comes

living with big dogs

Take special care if you live with both mini-sized and maxi-sized canines. Make clear rules and keep them. Don't let the dogs take each other's toys, and don't tolerate snapping or growling from either dog. A scene that would be a minor squabble between canine siblings can become a calamity when one dog is large and the other is small.

Even if your dainty dog and your big bruiser are best buddies, don't leave them loose together when they're unsupervised. All it takes is a misplaced paw or an out-of-control skid when you're gone, and you'll return home to tragedy.

from those few minutes he spent with Sarge, where he learned in silent doggie language that he wasn't the toughest dog on the block, but also learned that it's okay. If you have a kind, gentle, extremely safe big dog that can teach your puppy the same lesson, it can be a lifelong gift for your small dog.

PUPPY KINDERGARTEN

When I was a kid, human children didn't usually go to kindergarten; now it's considered an important part of their academic development. When I started training dogs, we didn't teach them anything until they were six months old. Now

we know that the best time for them to begin learning and socializing is at about three or four months of age. Puppy kindergartens have bloomed all over the country. This can be a great start for your puppy, if the trainer is sensitive to the needs of a small-sized dog.

Puppy classes usually teach very basic obedience. These classes should be happy, fun, and motivational, which means no choke collars, force, and never, ever pushing a puppy on his hips to make him sit or down.

Puppy kindergartens also usually have time for the dogs to play together. This shouldn't be a free-for-all. Left to their own devices, the bigger, stronger puppies sometimes terrorize the smaller, shier ones. Look for classes in

Puppy kindergarten can be a great start for your pet, but check out the class ahead of time.

which two puppies are paired together at a time, matched up for size and temperament. Don't go to a class where a boisterous puppy is allowed to overwhelm a smaller or shier one. Classes need to be kept under control, and no puppy should be mugging or scaring another.

Before you consider enrolling your puppy in a class, visit the class and see the instructor's techniques. Make sure that puppy play is appropriate and fun for all sizes and shapes of dogs and that all the training is positive and motivational.

Rescue Dogs

Remember the poster that used to proclaim, "It's never too late to have a happy childhood?" You'll find that if you adopt an older dog, it's never too late to give him a happy puppyhood. In fact, rescue dogs almost always figure out that they've been saved from whatever sad circumstances brought them to your door. While a well-bred, well-adjusted puppy is wonderful, there's an equally amazing magic to a dog who has faced some rough spots and found you to help him through.

Some rescue dogs will walk into the house and act as if they've lived there all their lives. The adjustment will be almost seamless. Others are a little more challenging. Happily, the gentle methods outlined in this book will help you address those challenges.

AGGRESSION

Shelter workers have told me many times that they'll adopt out a small dog with aggressive behaviors when they might euthanize a big dog with the same habits. Think carefully before bringing an aggressive dog, even a small one, into your home if you have children. The quick and unpredictable movements of a child make it hard for the aggressive dog to learn to control himself, and a dog that might bite isn't a fun pet for a kid.

If you have an adult home and you fall in love with the dog, take the chance on rehabilitating him if you're willing to work with him. Review the leadership sections of this book, as well as the problem solving section. If you need help, ask the shelter or rescue organization to recommend a trainer or behaviorist that uses positive methods to help you with the special needs of this rescue dog.

SHYNESS

Shyness and cautiousness are very common in rescue dogs. Your reassuring role as leader of the pack, combined with the confidence a dog gains in learning obedience skills, will take your shy little guy a long way. (For further reading, check out my other book, *Help for Your Shy Dog: Turning Your Terrified Dog into a Terrific Pet.*)

renaming your rescue dog

If you want to give your dog a new start in life, you might want to rename him. If you do it right, your new dog will love the process. Rename him the same way that you teach a puppy his name. With some treats, praise, and tummy scratches, your dog will think his new name is the best word on earth!

BELIEVE IN YOUR DOG

Dogs pick up what we think, whether it's some kind of psychic connection or just body language. If you have a dog who has had a sad history, acknowledge it but don't dwell on it. See your dog's happy future and current support in crystal-clear, technicolor vision. Your dog will begin to relax and share that sense of well-being with you.

Dogs are among the most resilient creatures on earth. When you see an abandoned, neglected, or even abused dog learn to trust, it will make your heart sing. When you see a fearful dog choose to be brave, you will be inspired. These dogs may need special time and patience, but isn't that what our relationships with our dogs are all about? If we were practical people, we'd only have dogs to herd our sheep or hunt for our food. Instead, we choose to have small dogs because they epitomize the relationship, rapport, and love that exist in that magical bond between humans and dogs.

Fun With Older Dogs

The magic of our relationships with our dogs only intensifies as they grow older. Happily, we can do a lot with training and activities to keep that connection with us for many years. Research has proven that we age more slowly if we're mentally and physically active. Activities are even a way to protect your older dog against canine cognitive dysfunction, an Alzheimer's-like disease.

Small-breed dogs outlive their larger cousins. The average life span of a 10-pound dog is twice that of a 200-pound dog. Many small dogs can be very active well into their teens.

Of course, keep your older dog's physical needs in mind while you work and play with him. If he seems to have even mild hip or back problems, don't ask him to jump. If his vision isn't what it used to be, stay close to him. But a few limitations shouldn't stop you from having a lot of fun.

Practice your obedience together. Play games, teach your dog tricks, laugh together, and go places together. Don't assign your senior dog to the couch just because he's reached a certain birthday. The adage, "You can't teach an old dog new tricks" was written about humans—not dogs.

Pekingese

chapter 3

Food, Fun, and Results

*M*odern, positive dog training rewards dogs for good behavior. Some people are resistant to giving their pooch a cookie. These people want the dog to do the command because he loves them, or because he's supposed to behave—period. The reality is that studies have proved that dogs learn fastest when they have a reward. This shouldn't be too surprising, because people are the same way. We expect to be paid for our work, and money is a hugely motivating reward for us humans. Money isn't the only reward that matters—we work harder when someone we respect praises us. Even when we were in school, A grades became a reward of their own—many of us worked very hard just to see that neat row of straight A's—and we felt happy and proud when we accomplished it.

Money, public recognition, a better office, a trophy, a company car—all of these motivate people to work hard and feel good about what they do. In the same vein, treats, lavish praise, petting in a favorite spot, a special toy—all of these can motivate a dog. This book will teach you how to use those motivational tools in a way that will reward your dog for good behavior and keep him having a tail-wagging good time.

Even if you wanted to, training a small dog with physical force doesn't make any sense. A small dog's delicate throat can be permanently damaged with a jerk on a choke collar. His spine and hips can be seriously injured if you pull up sharply on his collar or push on his rump to teach a sit. Besides, once you've tried training a dog using motivational methods, you'll never, ever want to go back to the "bad old days" of choke collars, leash jerking, and physical force.

Establishing Rapport

There are several things you can do to improve your small dog's behavior and to deepen your relationship with your four-footed family member that take almost no time or effort. These small acts will demonstrate to your dog, in doggie terms, that you are a leader. Your dog will learn to adore you even more than he did before. He'll also learn to relax. The techniques in this section are all extremely gentle and positive. Good leaders don't yell, scream, or hurt anyone. They provide a framework for living that makes the dog feel secure.

Interestingly, these techniques work on all dogs. Brash, pushy, aggressive dogs relax and become nicer, calmer dogs. Shy, fearful dogs relax and become bolder. These little steps are the closest things to magic that any dog trainer (that's you!) can offer.

Watch Me

"Watch me" may be the most important lesson you teach your dog. A dog who is looking at you can't get in a fight with another dog; it's physically impossible. It takes eye contact for your dog to chase a car, bark at a cat, or become aggressive with a big dog. If your dog is staring at your eyes, he can't create any trouble for himself. The watch me command also makes all other obedience infinitely easier to teach. A dog who is looking at you is more likely to learn what you are teaching him, just as kids in school are more likely to learn when they watch their teacher.

TEACHING WATCH ME

Hold a treat between your eyes and say, "Watch me." The dog will stare at you longingly. Well, he'll stare at the treat, but because the treat is between your eyes, he'll be focusing in your direction.

Instantly say, "Good watch me!" and reward the dog with the treat.

After the dog is looking at you consistently, hold the treat in your hand (out of sight of the dog). Say, "Watch me." If he looks at you, say, "Good watch me!" and reward him. If he looks at your hand, say, "Uh-uh, watch me." If he looks at your face, reward him. If he doesn't understand, then hold the treat in front of your eyes again and remind him of what you want.

your *misspent youth...*

If you ever played Indian Poker during your rowdy college years, holding the treat to your forehead may bring back some memories. In the poker game, you hold a card on your forehead and watch the other player's expressions as you decide how to bet. It's certainly more wholesome to have a happy dog staring lovingly at your face than a bunch of boisterous college kids.

Over time, mix up holding treats in front of your eyes and having a treat in your hand until you eventually always have the treat in your hand. Require the dog to look at you for longer periods of time before giving the reward. Practice "watch me" several times a day, always with a food reward!

PLAY CATCH

Once your dog has mastered "watch me," it's fun to teach him "catch." Playing catch also rewards your dog for paying attention to you.

To teach "catch," hold a treat just an inch over your dog's head and say, "Catch!" If the treat drops to the ground, quickly pick it up and try again. The only time your dog gets the treat is when he catches it in mid-air. Do this several times, and most dogs will be catching mid-air in a matter of minutes. Over time, drop the treat from higher and higher distances.

Note: Some dogs never get the hang of catch, since it takes a certain amount of depth perception and eye-mouth coordination that some dogs just don't have. Others never seem to get past their reaction to something (even a treat!) falling out of the sky toward their heads. Every dog can learn the watch me command—playing catch is just a bonus command that's fun for the majority of dogs.

Watch me (and catch for the dogs who enjoy the game) is extremely practical. The next time your pup wants to yap at that nasty dog down the street, you can just say, "Watch me!" Your dog will focus on you, and the problem will be resolved.

Playing a gentle game of catch can reinforce "watch me" and is fun for you and your dog.

These simple commands do something more profound as well. Once you teach them to your dog, your relationship may dramatically improve in a matter of days. He'll be looking to you for leadership and fun. You're becoming someone he wants to follow around, and that's the first step in strengthening the bond between the two of you.

Gentle Leadership

Dogs need humans to be their leaders. If we don't lead them, bossy dogs become unbearable; shy dogs become petrified. The biggest gift you can give to your dog, and to your relationship with him, is to be a kind, gentle, consistent leader.

If humans don't act like leaders, dogs become very stressed and anxious. Imagine how tough life is for a little dog who doesn't think you know how to lead the household. If you aren't acting like a leader (from a dog's perspective), he thinks you don't know how to take care of him. He believes that he can't count on you. If he goes to the vet's office, he needs to decide what he'll allow the vet to do, because he doesn't trust you to make that choice. If a strange person wants to pet him, he has to decide to allow it, to run, or to fight, because he doesn't think you have the ability to make those decisions for him. When people come to the house, he thinks he needs to decide whether to let them in and decide where they'll sit.

looking at food through a dog's eyes

When you first teach your dog the watch me command, he isn't really watching you. He's watching the yummy treat you're holding between your eyes. It's easy to dismiss the importance of what you're teaching your dog with this technique.

All dogs need leadership, and small dogs (and remember, they really do know they're small) crave it most of all. In doggie terms, the creature who has control of the food is the leader. So, at first your dog is looking in your eyes and thinking, "I just want the treat! NOW!" But soon the treat disappears from your face, and he's still staring lovingly at the spot where you once held the treat. He's transferred his feelings about the treat to you as a leader.

Humans do much the same thing when they feel warm and personally close to people who are rich, powerful, or famous. That treat in your face translates to you seeming powerful and rich, in doggie terms.

If you aren't a leader, a bold dog will take over the house. He's likely to become a barker and possibly a growler and nipper. But no matter what these dogs do, they never feel truly safe and secure. Even they know there's something wrong when the 7-pound dog is running the house. It's even worse for shy dogs who can experience round-the-clock panic if they don't think there's a strong leader in the house to protect them.

CANINE LEADERSHIP 101: WHAT TO DO EVERY DAY

1. Don't free-feed your dog. Give him two meals a day (three or four meals during puppyhood). In doggie terms, the lead dog is in charge of food, so this subtlety tells your dog that you're in charge. This simple bit of advice can do more to change your dog's behavior than any other single thing you can do. It's so simple, yet every single dog on earth will respond to it. For many dogs, it transforms a relationship.

Not only is this a great idea in terms of behavior; it's good for the health of your little dog. It gives you a chance to monitor his eating habits, which can be the first sign of illness, and it gives you control over his weight. Every dog should be fed at specific meal times, unless a veterinarian has a specific reason for recommending free-feeding your dog.

a lesson from goldie

My oldest Papillon is a 12-year-old named Goldie. I got her when she was two years old, and she was the shyest dog I'd ever met. She shook violently every time we left the small condominium I lived in at the time.

I'd worked for years in social services and knew that humans were happiest when they had the ability to make simple choices in their lives. It gave them a sense of control. So, without consciously thinking about it, I did the same for Goldie. If we came to a fork in the road on our walks, I'd ask her which way she wanted to go. I'd let her decide how close to come to strangers. Poor Goldie paid the price for me not thinking like a dog. In her mind, she was doomed. The 6-pound dog was in charge, and things didn't look good in this pack!

Once I realized my mistake, I took charge of our walks. I decided, not Goldie, which direction we'd go. I'd decide whether or not to let the person we met on the way pet her. Of course, I looked for every sign that Goldie gave me. She'd tell me which route she wanted to take on the walk and which people she liked better than others. She always got what she wanted, but it was my decision, not hers.

Within a week, our walks had transformed. She was no longer shaking; in fact, to this day, Goldie's very favorite thing in the world is to go for long walks, and I decide the route. She still lets me know her preferences, and I still listen every time. Goldie goes for her walks with a doggie smile and a wagging tail, confident that her loving, kind leader will safely lead the pack.

You don't have to be violent or even raise your voice to be a leader. You just have to convey leadership in dog terms.

2. Require your dog to sit, down, or do a trick before he gets a treat or his dinner. This subtly reinforces to your dog that you're in charge of the food. He'll be happy, even proud, to do his little job before being fed. If your pooch is overly pushy, growls at you, or ignores commands that he knows well, you should require him to sit, down, or do a trick before you pet him. Again, this tells him that you're in control of the space.

3. You decide when the dog is allowed on the bed. Teach him "on" and "off" the bed. When you get in bed, tell him "off" and (if you want to sleep with him) tell him he can get back on. The head dog determines who sleeps where.

4. Tell him, "Wait" at doorways. Always go through in front of him. I have a little pack of three Papillons: 12-year-old Goldie, 8-year-old Radar, and 3-year-old Pogo. From the day he came to the house, Pogo has declared himself head of the group. When I call the dogs inside when they've been playing in the backyard, it's fun to see Pogo fly through the door, sometimes jostling the other dogs out of his way. Why does he do that? Because the head dog goes through doors first. It's his way of telling his housemates that he's the leader. That's fine with me, but I insist that Pogo wait for me when I tell him to. After all, I'm Pogo's leader.

Like a child, your small dog looks to you for guidance and leadership.

These exercises don't add a minute to the time you spend with your dog every day, and they don't take any special equipment or training. I promise you that if you: 1) give your dog meals; 2) have him sit (or do another trick) when you feed him or give him attention; 3) decide when and where he sleeps; and 4) tell him to wait at doors, you'll have a calmer, more tractable dog who will be a nicer, happier dog to live with—I guarantee it.

Gentle Restraint: Gaining Control in an Instant

Sometimes your dog, especially if he's a rowdy adolescent, gets out of control. He'll squirm in your arms, making it clear he has *much* better things to do than hang out with you. He may not let you put on his collar, or he might even growl or snap. In most cases, the worst way to react is to yell at or try to manhandle your dog; you'll just end up in a battle of wills. And no mere human being has ever successfully won a battle of wills with a small dog. Even if you win the physical war, your goal is to have a gentle, loving, trusting relationship with your dog. You lose that relationship when you resort to yelling and violence to control your dog.

The answer is a simple technique called *Gentle Restraint*. Gentle restraint teaches your dog patience. It's easy to use gentle restraint on a small dog, because you can envelop his entire body with your arms, lap, and torso.

Hold the dog gently, but solidly, in your arms until he stops squirming. You aren't squeezing him tightly, and you aren't struggling with him. You're simply supporting his body in a way that immobilizes him. He'll figure out that squirming around isn't doing him any good.

When you feel his muscles relax and his breathing slow, say in a calm voice, "Good settle." As soon as he's settled in your arms for a second, tell him he was a good dog, and release him to play.

Gentle restraint is not a battle of wills, and this isn't holding a dog so tightly that he can hurt himself. This is just a way of communicating to your dog that he earns more freedom when he practices self-restraint than when he doesn't.

I've seen gentle restraint used effectively on people, in a much tougher environment. Years ago, I was the executive director of an agency that runs housing and chemical dependency treatment programs, primarily for homeless people. The agency operates the alcohol and drug detox programs for the Portland area. The staff has an absolute commitment to nonviolence, even though they are often working with people who have been brought in under police custody from situations such as bar fights. On the rare occasions that a client in detox decided to act violently, the staff was trained just to fall gently on top on the person. Their bodies made violence impossible and allowed the intoxicated person to calm down. If this technique works for intoxicated people under police custody, it can certainly work for your 10-pound dog!

Remember to always tell the dog that he's good the moment he settles down, and release him to play when he is acting calm.

Touching, Touching, Touching!

Recently, a friend of mine who works in a veterinary hospital was very upset. In the previous week, two dogs had come into the clinic that were too aggressive to handle safely. Both of these dogs were in the late stages of cancer. Sadly, no one had felt safe touching and examining these dogs when their disease was in the early, treatable stages.

These dogs' deaths may have been hastened because they wouldn't sit calmly for touching. Even if touching isn't a life and death matter for your dog, it does impact the quality of his life. Your dog needs to be comfortable and calm when he's being examined by his veterinarian, when he goes to the groomer, or when a friend pets him. Toy and small-breed dogs are held and handled more than their larger cousins; life is miserable for them if they don't learn to enjoy or at least complacently tolerate touching.

scamp lessons

Scamp is a young Beagle with a mind of his own. Owners Marilyn and Bill were trying to keep up with touching him all over, but admit it didn't always make their "to-do" list. They were more than busy trying to teach Scamp to walk calmly on his leash during neighborhood outings, sit and stay, and not bark for attention.

Then Scamp got a minor ear infection, and Marilyn and Bill, of course, promptly took him to the vet for treatment. That's when they realized they had a problem on their hands. Scamp refused to let the veterinary staff examine or treat him, and he made everyone think he'd bite them. They muzzled him to complete the exam.

Scamp is not an aggressive or vicious dog, but he is a clever one. He realized that he got his way when he snapped. Marilyn decided this wasn't what she wanted for her young dog, and began touching Scamp all over, rewarding him for good behavior. She can now lift his lip and show his teeth without a problem. Her work with this dog will pay off for years to come!

If you put yourself in your dog's paws, you'll realize it can be hard. Human hands are big to a little dog, and just imagine how large the hypodermic needle at the vet's office must seem. Still, with persistence, calm handling, and a positive attitude, even a shy dog can learn to calmly accept petting and even veterinary poking and prodding.

LIFT UP

You can't physically examine a small dog unless he's on your lap, in your arms, or on a table. The first challenge is to get the dog off the floor. Remember, it must be terrifying to be a 5-pound dog and suddenly feel a hand come down and swoop you up into the air. If humans faced this kind of scary scenario, Hitchcock could have made a movie about it.

You can eliminate your dog's fear of being lifted up by telling him what you're doing. Just say, "Lift up!" every single time you pick him up. Sometimes, just give him a treat or a gentle hug and put him back down.

Be sure to fully support your dog's body when you lift him up. It can physically hurt your dog's spine and ribs if you don't cradle both his front and rear in your arms as you pick him up. If being lifted up is painful, he will become even more afraid of being held.

You'll notice that your dog will start to set himself for you to pick him up when you say, "Lift up!" Respect what he's telling you about the way he wants you to pick him up. One dog might hold himself rigid on all four paws, while another one might put his paws up on your knees. Work together with your dog to make this a safe, comfortable, enjoyable moment together.

BODY PARTS

Imagine how scary your own annual physical would be if your physician didn't warn you that he or she was about to poke, pinch, or grab an intimate area. You'd probably consider biting your doctor. You're able to accept the procedure because you know what's coming next. You can teach your dog what's coming next in his exam, as well. Teach him the names of his body parts. When you touch your dog, give him treats, saying, "Good nose!" or "Good feet!" Over time, he'll associate being touched, even in delicate areas, with a happy experience.

Teach him names for his eyes, ears, feet, nose, tail, teeth, tummy, and rear end. Start out with a gentle touch and a quick food reward. For example, just touch his toes gently, saying, "Good feet!" and give him a favorite treat.

t-shirts that tame

Tellington Touch (also called T-Touch) is a system of extremely light massage that has a long-lasting, calming effect on animals. Most of the moves are very light, circular motions on the dog's skin. The theory behind T-Touch is that it programs away trauma and fear from the dog's nervous system.

Many small dogs are very tightly wired. They tend to shake or to be so busy that they don't connect easily with their humans. If your dog tends to be tense, shy, or hyperactive, this gentle form of touching might make an enormous difference in his life.

One technique that Tellington-Jones recommends is to put worried dogs in T-shirts. Having their torsos surrounded by fabric sometimes has an extremely calming effect on dogs. Obviously, your small breed dog won't fit in an adult's T-shirt. (I once made temporary T-shirts for my Goldie and Radar out of the arms of a T-shirt and even that was too big for Goldie!) Check out T-shirts for toddlers, infants, or even premies for your small dogs

To learn more about T-Touch, check out the many books, videos, and classes by Linda Tellington-Jones and the people who have studied with her. Many libraries carry the books and videos, and they are easily available for purchase on-line. Learn more at www.lindatellington-jones.com.

As he's comfortable with his body parts being touched lightly, make the exam more probing, as it would be at the veterinarian's. For example, after your dog calmly accepts having his feet touched lightly, begin to gently examine between the pads of his feet. After he's accepted having his muzzle touched, begin to look at his front teeth, and later his back teeth. Always make this touching fun. It's a happy time between the two of you. Ask other people to touch your dog as well, and have them give your dog the treat.

Yorkshire Terrier

Luring, Learning, and Communicating

Training a small dog is a little bit like driving a sports car. These dogs are easy to maneuver, and they're tons of fun. Our little dogs are also more sensitive and may need a little more finesse than the doggie equivalent of a station wagon or a minivan. It's vital to train your dog in a way that makes him feel safe, that can't hurt his sometimes delicate body, and that is fun for both dog and human. There are two types of positive training techniques: clicker training and lure and reward training.

Clicker Training

A clicker is a little hand-held, low-tech device with a metal strip that makes a sharp, distinctive *click* when you push it. Dogs learn to recognize that the *click* is a magically good thing, because you pair the *click* with a food reward—Click, treat; Click, treat. Within minutes every dog loves to hear the click. After the dog understands that a click means good things, the clicker is used to highlight good behavior. The instant that the dog does something that you like, you click the behavior.

Debi Davis has trained her tiny Papillon dogs to be her service dogs, helping out with tasks that are difficult for her to do from a wheelchair, including picking up pens, coins, and even newspapers from the floor; pulling the laundry out of the dryer; bringing the phone; helping to make the bed; and opening and shutting drawers, cabinets, and doors.

She's done all this training with a clicker. She explains, "Think of a camera click—that clicking sound captures a moment in time."

Lure and Reward Training

Lure and reward training hasn't gotten all the press that clicker training has received, but it is equally positive. It's the primary technique that most competitive dog trainers use and is the method used in this book.

In this method, a lure (such as a yummy treat) helps the dog find the position that you want. For example, if you want your dog to sit, you move the treat over his head, and he follows the treat with his nose until he automatically sits. You've lured him into place with the treat, and you'll reward him with it when he does what you want him to do.

Lure and reward training uses treats to elicit and reward desired behaviors.

If you're a theorist, the lure and reward method gently, non-violently gets the dog to do what you want and then rewards the behavior. Clicker training waits for the dog to offer the behavior and then *clicks* the behavior to set it in the dog's mind. Theoretically, the click replaces the word, "Good!" and trainers should be unemotional.

For people who aren't so theoretical, both methods can be combined. For example, if you want to click your dog, just substitute a click when the instructions in this book tell you to say, "Good!" The training style in this book is a little emotional, in that it's fun, smiling, happy, cheering. Whether you want to click or lure and reward, I think your dog will do best when you're smiling and encouraging him.

Say It With Meaning

One of the greatest dog training lessons of all time is a *The Far Side* cartoon. A man is looking at his dog, obviously angry; the dog is expressionless, serene. The caption says, "What we say to dogs." The guy is pointing at the dog, shouting, "Okay, Ginger! I've had it! You stay out of the garbage! Understand, Ginger? Stay out of the garbage, or else!"

The next caption says, "What they hear." The picture is identical, but the words say, "Blah blah, Ginger! Blah blah blah blah blah blah blah blah, Ginger, blah blah blah blah blah!"

Of course, the cartoon is just plain funny, but it also underlines the fact that we expect our dogs to understand everything we say, without ever giving them the information they need to learn from us.

The truth is that while Ginger won't ever understand the diatribe about the garbage, she can learn to understand and respond to hundreds of words. (Okay, Ginger is a cartoon dog and won't really learn anything. But your dog can!)

The key is to tie every action you want to train your dog with a specific word. If you want your dog to come to you, say, "Ginger, here!" or "Come!"—or, as one student of mine once did, "Grapes!" Which word you choose isn't important. It does matter that it is always consistent and always means the same thing. So, if "Come!" means come running and sit at your feet, don't sometimes say, "Here" and sometimes, "Haul your body to me." For your dog to understand what you want, you need to use the same word for the same action every single time. It's also important that you don't give one word two different meanings. If "down" means "lie down," it shouldn't also mean, "Get off the couch."

dogs don't understand abstractions

I was in an obedience class once when one of the other participants said to her dog, "That was great," after her dog made a mistake. The instructor pointed out that the dog had done the exercise incorrectly, not "great."

The woman answered indignantly, "I was being ironic."

Dogs don't understand irony. "Good" really always has to mean "good." Similarly, dogs don't understand negatives, so don't say, "Don't jump!" or "Don't bark!" All the dog hears is "Blah, blah, blah jump! Blah, blah, blah bark!"

The more you use words, the more your dog will understand and feel comfortable in his environment. Use "walk" when you want to go out for a walk, and "car" when you're going for a ride. Tell him "breakfast" and "dinner" are ready, and give him "treats" when he's good. The more you use specific words repeatedly, the more your dog can cooperate. Many dogs learn that words have meaning and pick up on the words that you use in conversation. I have a friend whose dog loves to chase squirrels. She uses the word "gorilla" instead of squirrel, because her dog turns into a screaming banshee when she hears the word "squirrel," even in a conversational tone.

Use specific words to teach your dog things—he'll pick up on their meaning.

It's My Name: Don't Wear It Out

There are a nearly infinite number of words in the English language. Add to that all the words from other languages, and even some you can make up for yourself, and you'd think it would be easy to name everything you want your dog to do. Unfortunately, most people don't seem to use words when they're asking their dogs to do something: They just say the poor dog's name.

"Ginger!" means, "Come!"

"Ginger!" means, "Get off the sofa!"

"Ginger!" means, "Stay!"

"Ginger!" means, "I'm home – greet me!"

"Ginger!" means, "Bad, bad, bad dog!"

"Ginger!" means, "I love you, you sweet dog!"

Poor Ginger, it's no wonder she never does what her human wants her to do. She has no idea what it is. How could she?

How well would you perform at work if:

"Deborah!" (*insert your name here*) meant, "Get the information on the new account!"

"Deborah!" meant, "Let's go to lunch!"

"Deborah!" meant, "Turn the lever to the *left* at the nuclear power plant!"

"Deborah!" meant, "Turn the lever to the *right* at the nuclear power plant!"

Obviously, you couldn't do your job; you wouldn't have enough information to perform the right task at the right time. The same is true for your dog. How does she know that this time when you say, "Ginger!" you want her to sit and stay, but next time you want her to come to you?

Listen to yourself. If you find yourself repeating your dog's name, you aren't giving her the information that he needs to succeed.

How Dogs Learn

Learning using a lure and reward method is a five-step process:

1. You will lure the dog into a behavior.

2. Through repetition (made fun with the lure) the dog will figure out what you want in the behavior.

3. Once the dog understands the exercise, the lure turns into a reward.

4. You will re-teach the exercise in different places until the dog learns it.

5. The dog will forget and re-learn the exercise as the behavior goes from short-term memory to long-term memory.

Leave out any step and your dog won't permanently learn what you want him to. Let's go over those steps one at a time, because they're the foundation to success and communication with your dog!

1. **Lure the dog into a behavior.** When you teach a dog to sit by putting a cookie in front of his nose, he's just following the cookie. He doesn't know that folding his back legs and putting his butt on the ground is a sit. (Remember, he doesn't speak English.)

   The higher the level of reward, the easier it is to lure him into the behavior. It's easier to get his nose to move to a bite of steak than for a piece of kibble.

2. **Through repetition (made fun with the lure) the dog will figure out what you want in the behavior.** Your dog will make a connection between getting the treat and the action of his butt hitting the floor. He'll have a little "aha!" moment and will volunteer the behavior. Your dog has used his power of reasoning to determine the behavior you wanted!

3. **Once the dog understands the exercise, the lure turns into a reward.** The treat now comes after the exercise. On the sit, you'll hold the treat in your hand, say, "Sit," and then give the dog his reward. To test whether or not the dog really understands the exercise, try it without the lure. For the sit, hold the treat in your hand, and say, "Sit." If he understands, great! Reward him with the treat. If he doesn't understand, help him by luring him into place and then giving him the treat.

Once the dog knows the behavior, begin to give variable and unpredictable rewards. Sometimes it will be just "Good boy," sometimes it will be a scratch on the butt, sometimes it will be a game with a favorite toy, and sometimes it will be food. Part of the fun for the dog is to see what nice thing happens when he does his work. It's important for the dog to receive variable and unpredictable rewards or else the treat becomes something he's *entitled* to every time. That's when you have a person calling, "Come, Ginger!" and Ginger gently wrinkles her nose, determines the person has no treat, and walks away. Variable and unpredictable rewards keep the human in the equation.

4. **You will re-teach the exercise in different places until the dog learns it.** Dogs don't generalize what we've taught them. If he's always done his stay 3 feet away, he might not be able to do it 6 feet away. If you've always practiced indoors, he might not understand what you want when you're outside. Be patient and re-train the dog in different places and under slightly different conditions.

If your dog makes a mistake twice in a row, he's telling you he doesn't understand what you're asking. Go back a step and make it easier for him. If you need to lure him into place again, fine; if you need to be closer, fine. Do whatever your dog needs to understand what you're asking, then gradually make the exercise more difficult again.

5. **The dog will forget and re-learn the exercise as the behavior goes from short-term memory to long-term memory.** For example, your dog will be doing the exercise perfectly for you. Life is good. Suddenly, one day you will ask him to do

Laugh, tell your dog he's brilliant, and have a good time together.

the command, and he won't be able to do it. You'll look in his face and see that it's full of confusion.

Don't panic! This is a normal stage of learning for dogs. The theory is that dogs lose access to the information as it goes from short-term to long-term memory. Just gently and patiently re-teach the command. The dog will re-learn it in a fraction of the time it took to learn it in the first place. (My dog, Radar, always looks so upset during this process of unlearning a command. He's such a good, willing boy, and you can just see his face saying, "I *know* I used to know that word! What's happening to my brain?" When he re-learns it, you can see the look of joy on his face.) Once your dog has gone through this process, he knows the exercise and will perform it reliably.

Keep it fun—this isn't grim; this isn't punishment. This is your special, delightful, fun time together. Enjoy it! Communicate, laugh, tell your dog he's brilliant. You'll both have a great time. Remember, dog training is about communicating with each other, not merely about doing a reliable command. Now, let's start training your dog!

Maltese

Five Must-Know Behaviors

A dog or a human can't learn everything at once. This section outlines the five basic exercises every dog needs to learn: sit, stay, come, walk on a loose lead, and down. Your dog doesn't have to learn all of these the first day. Concentrate on learning one or two exercises a week. When I teach classes, we usually learn sit and watch me the first week; practice come and walking on a loose leash the second week; start working on down the third week; and hone our stay skills the fourth week—then work on solidifying those skills over the next seven weeks.

Small dogs are the longest-living canines. Most little ones live to be 14 or so with a little luck, and many small dogs live to be 18 and older. Give your dog a little time and don't rush things too much. Relax and enjoy learning together.

#1. Sit

Pop quiz time! Do you remember when we taught your dog watch me? If you cheated and skipped that chapter, go review it (Chapter 2). It will make your task infinitely easier if you have a dog who loves to look adoringly into your eyes.

This is the easiest method to teach sit and is perfect for every well-behaved pet.

- Hold a treat in front of your dog's nose.

- Slowly pull the treat over the dog's head, between the dog's ears. Almost all dogs will naturally rock back into a sit.

- Say, "Good sit!" and give the reward while the dog is in the sitting position.

- If the dog doesn't automatically sit, *gently* tuck your finger under his rear to help him go into a sit position.

- If your dog is turning around, you might want to practice in a confined space. Put him on a comfortable chair where he feels safe. He'll back up to the back of the chair, and then you can lure him into a sit.

- If you notice that your dog is doing a "sit up and beg" position, it means you're holding the treat too high. Hold it just above his nose.

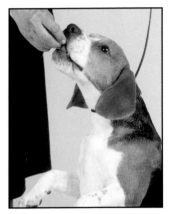

Always reward your dog when he's doing what you want him to do.

Important: Don't *ever* push down on your dog's rear end to make him sit. It can damage any dog and can easily permanently injure a small breed puppy's hips and back. Don't ever pinch his kidneys (as some trainers show you), as this can potentially harm him internally. Let the treat do the work; your dog will figure it out. Just be patient and let him take his time. If you're thinking about competing in obedience trials with your dog (yes, small dogs can beat the big boys, and there are opportunities for mixed breeds to compete), there's a slightly different way to teach the sit that will result in higher scores, which is discussed later in the book.

#2. Stay

Before you even think about practicing stay with your dog, there's an important concept to memorize: *Always* give your dog the reward when he's doing what you ask him to do! Most people teach their dogs the "un-stay." They say, "Stay! Stay there, boy. Good stay!" The good little dog keeps his butt on the ground and doesn't move a muscle. Finally, the time is up; the little dog succeeded in his stay! What does the trainer do? She releases the dog and then rewards him. So what does the dog learn? That he gets rewarded when he gets up!

When your dog is doing a sit-stay (or any other command), reward him while he's doing what you want. The dog will understand much more quickly

why teach "sit" first?

There's a reason why almost every dog trainer starts with teaching sit—dogs learn it incredibly quickly and easily. Within a matter of a few minutes, almost every dog, young or old, rescue or show dog, will be sitting on command. Because it's so common, it's easy to miss the pure magic of this moment. Your dog has just crossed the chasm between the other animals and humans; understanding what you asked him to do, he did it. It is from this first moment of true communication that so much more will grow.

what you want him to do, and he will become patient, waiting for the reward he knows will be coming to him if he stays still. If you reward a dog consistently while he stays still, then he'll learn to love to do a sit-stay. (Note: Be sure your dog knows and understands sit before you start. Sit and stay are two different commands.)

- After you tell your dog, "Sit," take a step back about 6 inches and gently say, "Stay, good sit-stay." Instantly, and while he is still sitting, reward him. He can't learn to sit for one minute until he's learned to sit for one second.

- When he succeeds at a one-second sit-stay, expand the time to five seconds, ten seconds, etc. If he consistently gets up after (for example) 15 seconds, give him a 12-second stay and reward him. Help him succeed.

- Chain together two or more stays. Tell him, "Stay" and reward after 10 seconds, then step back and tell him, "Stay" and reward him after another 15 seconds.

TEACHING TECHNIQUES

Sadly, many people teach stay as if it's a horrendous punishment. As always, think about what this does to your dog. It's hard enough for a small dog to have the courage to sit and stay while you walk away; this exercise really teaches him to have trust and faith in you. Imagine how much harder it is for this little guy if you're screaming, "STAY! STAY! STAAAAAAAYYY!" Just relax and tell him how clever he is for staying, and you and the dog will do better.

Barbara Cecil is one of America's top dog trainers; among her top-

your ultimate goal

Advanced obedience dogs do out-of-sight stay exercises when they enter dog shows. All the dogs entered in the class line up together; a little Miniature Pinscher might be next to a Doberman Pinscher, or a Chihuahua might be next to a Great Dane. The judge orders the handlers to "leave your dogs," and the handlers leave the building. Dogs do a three-minute sit-stay. The handlers return to their dogs, then put the dogs on a five-minute down-stay and leave the building again. They're doing this exercise in the middle of a dog show, where there might be hundreds of other dogs, loudspeakers blaring, and kids eating hot dogs next to the obedience rings.

You may never want to enter a dog show, but think about training your dog to have just as reliable a sit-stay as the dogs who compete at trials. It's a great peace of mind to know that your dog will likely stay still no matter what, especially when there's an emergency. Remember, though, that five-minute, out-of-sight stay exercise started with a simple one-second stay. It's the way dogs learn.

winning obedience and agility dogs have been three Papillons and a Löwchen (a small, fluffy breed originally from Germany). Barbara tells people, "Teach stay as if it's a trick." What she means is that stay should be every bit as interesting and enjoyable for your dog as shaking hands, rolling over, or jumping for a treat. You don't scream and threaten your dog when he's learning the sit or come command, and there's no need to make stay anything but a fun accomplishment for your dog.

MAKING IT HARDER

It's harder for people to think when the environment is busy, and the same is true for dogs. Imagine yourself at the busiest mall at Christmas time. People are jostling all around you; carolers are singing; the Salvation Army Santa is ringing the bell; and kids are screaming. Now imagine being asked to do a complex math problem, recite the opening lines of Macbeth, or learn the symbols on the Periodic Table of Elements. Yikes! You'd be hard-pressed to do it.

Stay should be a fun accomplishment for your dog, not a punishing lesson.

If you were asked to do the same task at your desk at work or in the quiet of your living room, you might be able to do it in a snap. It's hard to perform complex tasks or to learn new things in busy places.

Remember this when training your dog. The more relaxed and familiar the environment is, the better your dog will perform. The more tense and busy it is, the worse he will do—just like humans.

If your dog is having trouble doing a task out in public that he does fine at home, don't be upset with him. Just take a step back and go forward from where he can succeed. Just because he can do a three-minute sit-stay in the security of his backyard doesn't mean he can do the same thing in a busy pet supply store. If he can't do three minutes, see if he can do one minute or thirty seconds. Find where he can succeed and go forward from there.

Releasing Your Dog

One of the hardest things for a dog is to know when an exercise is over. He's sitting by your side and watching you, watching you, watching you. You're talking with friends, enjoying yourself. At some point, your dog has to guess when the exercise is over. If he stops doing his task and you don't say anything, apparently he guessed right. If you get irked or put him back in place when he moves, apparently he guessed wrong. This isn't fair to your little dog.

Teach your dog a release word. When you say this word, your dog's exercise is finished. He can relax and do whatever he wants to do or do whatever you ask next.

SELECTING A RELEASE WORD

The most common release word is "okay!" I must admit I use this one, but it's not the best. A friend of mine described taking her five Border Collies to the vet. She was paying the bill after the dogs' exam; her highly trained dogs were sitting in a semi-circle around her. The receptionist told my friend the amount of the bill. "Okay," said my friend, and five Border Collies leapt up in unison, with the thought of bolting for the door. Because we say, "Okay" so often without realizing it in casual conversation, you might want to come up with another release word.

Any word or short phrase will do—"At ease!" "You're done!" "Off duty!"—any word that sticks well in your mind. I have one good friend who tells her Papillon, "Free dog!" The really hip people who herd with their Border Collies say, "That'll do" to release their dogs. I fantasize about saying, "That'll do" to my little dogs, who are just as cool as a Border Collie, as far as I'm concerned.

Don't use "Good!" or other words of praise as your release word. You want to tell your dog he's good in the middle of an exercise and still have him continue to stay, come, or sit. The release word must be separate and distinct in sound from "Good!"

Be sure to give your dog his release word at the end of every exercise, so he knows when it's done. It will make life easier for him and will also make him better able to follow the directions that you give him. He won't be standing up from his sit periodically just to see if the exercise is over. Clarity will help him do a better job.

#3. Come

The come command should be the most joyful, glorious, happy word your dog can hear. He needs to know that when he turns and runs to you that great and wonderful things will happen: treats, play, kisses, toys. When your dog is chasing a squirrel and you call him, he needs to know that it's more fun to come running to you than to chase the squirrel. (Yes, you have to be more interesting than a squirrel.)

failing to come

The number-one reason people sign up their small dogs for obedience class is because they fail to come on command.

The come command needs to be taught in an enclosed room or a completely fenced-in area. Put your dog on a long leash, but only use it to corral him if he decides to go running in circles and play "zoomies." *Don't* pull on the leash when you teach him this fun, energetic, lively command.

For the first few weeks, teaching "come" is a two-person job. Someone else needs to hold the dog while you walk away and call the dog. (If you're both in the same household, it's great to call the dog back and forth.) The person holding the dog should be *silent*. You should get the dog revved up, eager to come to you. In a high, happy voice, say, "Ready? Ready? Ready?" Then call him with a very clear "Come!" command.

Be very, very fun. Use a happy voice. Squat down and clap your hands or turn and run in the other direction. Make yourself interesting and appealing.

use a magic word

Use a magic word for "come." Perhaps you've spent the entire last year saying, "Come! I said come! This time I really mean it! Come! No, stop chasing the cat! I said come! This time I really, really mean it! Come! No—don't eat the couch! Come! This time I really, really, really mean it!" In this case, "come" isn't the best word to use any more. It certainly has no sense of magic to your dog.

Use "here," "front," or something cute and clever. Just don't use a word your dog has been ignoring for years.

When your dog comes to you, treat him and praise him for at least 15 seconds. When you come home, your dog doesn't just come up at say, "Good" in a monotone. He bounces up and down; he wiggles; he licks; he snuggles; and he says he's thrilled, just thrilled to see you. You need to show the same happiness when your dog comes to you on command. Your dog needs to know that you're excited that he came to you—so act like it!

Practice three times a day. Don't overdo this one, because you want to keep this a spontaneous, joyful communication between you and your dog.

KEEPING IT FUN

Don't ever call your dog to you for punishment or something even mildly unpleasant. If you need to clip your dog's nails, go collect him—don't call him. You want this command to represent only the good things. When your little dog sees a cat across the street and a car is coming, you want your dog to think it's better to come to you than to tear across the street after that cat. That won't happen if he thinks you're calling him to trim his nails.

During training, show your dog that coming when called will result in praise, encouragement, and lots of treats.

WHAT TO DO IF YOUR DOG DOESN'T COME

Most dogs respond to this happy calling with glee and run joyfully to their person. Occasionally, a dog has a mind of his own. He meanders off and sniffs the floor or goes running around the room madly. There is a solution that works almost every time, even for the most independent little dog.

Without getting upset, gather the dog's long leash and bring him right to you. Take his treat out of your pocket. (It's important to practice this command with a treat you find edible, such as string cheese or some meat.) Show the dog the treat he could have earned, and say, "Well, I get the treat."

Pop it in your mouth. Eat the treat like it's the best, most incredible morsel you've had in your life. Slurp noisily; smack your lips; say just how delicious it is; but don't you *dare* fake eating the treat. Eat it in front of the dog and swallow it. He'll get the message loud and clear: He just lost out on the most incredible reward of his lifetime because he didn't come to you.

Give the dog back to your friend to hold and show the dog the treat. Once again, call him enthusiastically, and I bet he'll come running. If he's the rare dog who doesn't, just repeat the process. With him sitting at your feet, you eat the treat with enormous gusto.

Give him back to your friend and call him a third time. I've never met a dog who didn't come the third time. When he comes, give him a big "jackpot" treat. Tell him he's great—make it incredibly worthwhile to come to you. Soon, you'll have a dog who's learned that coming is a very cool activity.

SEPARATING STAY FROM COME

It's tempting to teach the stay and come command together. After all, that's what you see trained dogs do all the time. The handler says, "Stay," walks across the room, and then calls the dog. What could be more sensible?

If you combine stay and come too soon, your dog will have trouble doing a reliable stay for weeks. Remember the "Dog Game" at the beginning of this book? Your dog is trying to figure out what you want, and he hasn't read the training book. When you say, "Stay," leave him, and then call him; within a few times he'll have this stay exercise figured out. What he concludes "stay" to mean is to sit still for about 30 seconds and then go running to his person.

motivating your dog

It seems counterintuitive, but the best way to attract your dog to come to you is to position yourself far across the room. If you're close, you're old hat. When you're across the room, he'll be a bit more anxious to come to you. Remember, this must be done in a safe, enclosed room or yard—don't take chances with your dog's life by hoping he'll learn to come in an open yard.

A reliable stay is a huge safety precaution for your dog. Don't jeopardize it by combining stay with come too early. In my class, I don't let students combine the commands until the dog has clearly understood and practiced both commands separately for at least three weeks. It's important to remember not to combine them too soon—it's for his safety.

#4. Walking on a Loose Leash

Wow! You've come this far, and you've already done a lot! Your dog does "watch me"—casting adoring eyes at you, rather than engaging in a verbal discussion with the dog next door. He welcomes, or at least tolerates, touch from other people. He sits, stays, and comes on command. You've covered the most important life-saving training. Congratulations! Now you can work on the behaviors that will simply make life with your pint-sized pooch more enjoyable.

Think about what walks with your dog are like. Is he pulling on the lead, maybe even choking himself in his efforts to go farther, faster? Or is he worried, even shaking, when you go places, hiding behind your ankles? In either case, he's not having very much fun, and certainly neither are you. Teaching your dog to walk calmly on a loose leash will be a gift for both of you. Happily, teaching your dog to walk calmly on a loose leash usually doesn't take very long.

TEACHING "LET'S GO!"

Your dog should be on a comfortable buckle or snap collar (not a choke collar) and you should have a lightweight 4-foot or 6-foot leash (not a Flexi leash).

- Say, "Let's go" (or "walkies" or whatever word suits you) and start walking.

- If he pulls, turn in the other direction and say, "Let's go!" the instant his leash tightens. If he runs out and pulls in the new direction, turn and go a different way, saying, "Let's go!" Repeat until you've tired him out. This may take several repetitions. Be patient, and don't give in or yank your dog.

don't be a "jerk!"

In the bad old days, we used to teach dogs to walk with us by jerking on the leash. This is a bad idea for any dog, and it's a terrible idea for a small dog, with his delicate neck. Don't "correct" your dog by pulling or jerking on his leash! When you turn directions, warn your dog by saying, "Let's go!" and showing him a treat or patting your lower leg. This exercise should teach your dog that it's fun to follow you, not painful!

- The *moment* he's moving on a loose leash, give him an easily chewed treat and tell him he's a very, very good dog. Very quickly, your dog will figure out that he will never, ever get where he wants to go if he pulls. On the other hand, keeping his eye on you is incredibly fun.

- Keep these lessons short at first so that neither of you get frustrated. Even on a loose leash, go just a short distance before rewarding your dog. Soon it will start working on every walk.

Teaching your dog to walk calmly on a loose leash will be a gift for both of you.

Of course, working in the living room or backyard is one thing; walking your dog on the street is another matter. Once you've really mastered "Let's go!" in a place with low distractions, practice it somewhere with more noises, smells, and activities. Even if you feel silly, do the same procedure as above. If you consistently and adamantly follow this procedure, your dog will be walking nicely with you within a week.

Yes, I know you can feel a bit dizzy changing directions several times, and you might be worried about what the neighbors will say. (But this certainly can't be the oddest thing they've seen you do!) But if you follow this technique for just a few days, you'll have a lifetime of happy, calm walks together.

TEACHING A SHY DOG "LET'S GO!"

While the busy, brash dogs are leading at the end of the leash, the shy ones are trailing behind at the end of theirs. Be gentle and patient with your shy dog. The more you are anxious and upset, the worse the problem becomes.

Practice in places where your shy dog feels comfortable: the living room, the yard, the sidewalk in front of your house. Give him whatever rewards he'll accept—food, happy scratches, or just listening to your calm, happy praise.

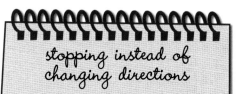

stopping instead of changing directions

Some dog trainers give a variation of the technique I've described. They suggest that you merely stop when the dog comes to the end of the leash and wait for him to calm down before going forward. You can always try this method (since it will make you a bit less dizzy than the one I use), but in my experience, it seldom works with small dogs. Why? Because they can amuse themselves mightily on just a leash-length. They circle, they jump, they bark. If you have a busy little dog—and that's usually the kind of dog who's at the end of a leash—you will need to change directions for him to realize that being in charge isn't as much fun as being a follower.

A big help for shy dogs is to practice with a bold one. Whenever I have a shy dog in class, I place him near a happy-go-lucky, confident little dog. Then we have the confident dog do the exercise first; he does it with a wagging tail. After a shy dog sees the bold dog do an exercise and sees that the bold dog lives through it, the shy one will be more likely to take the chance.

Don't ever force your shy dog to walk. Just give him the opportunity and reward, reward, reward every single step of progress.

USING A HEAD COLLAR

Head collars are designed similarly to the halters that fit on a horse's head. The theory is that the whole body of the dog follows his nose. Just as you can control a 1,500-pound horse with a head halter, you can do the same with a dog's head collar.

Very few small dogs I've worked with have needed a head collar. After all, it's not like you need a special gizmo to keep your dog under the most basic control. Small dogs almost always respond quickly to the technique of changing directions outlined in this chapter.

However, a head collar, even on a small dog, has helped in a few cases. These have mostly been cases in which the dog has been very much in charge of the household for some time, and walking on a leash had become a battle of wills. Happily, a head collar ends that battle of wills; the dog simply has to follow where you lead.

A head collar sometimes has a profound calming effect on some rowdy dogs. Lead dogs often greet a subordinate dog by gently nuzzling the top of the lower-ranked dog's muzzle. In doggie language, a gentle pressure across the top of the muzzle says that someone else is in charge. So, the whole time the dog is wearing a head collar, a part of his brain is telling him to relax, someone else is in charge—and it must be the human on the other end of the leash. Who knew?

If you decide to try a head collar:

- Be sure to get the right size. Although not all stores carry them, the majority of manufacturers make them even for teeny dogs.

- Ask someone knowledgeable to help you fit it on your dog. Properly fitted, they're comfortable, although a new experience for your dog. Improperly fitted, they can be too loose (allowing your dog to wriggle free) or too tight (which can be uncomfortable, even painful, on the dog's muzzle).

- Practice at home before you go outside with it, because some dogs wiggle and squirm to get out of them.

While most small dogs don't need these devices, it's worth trying one if your dog is really struggling with you when you're trying to walk him.

#5. Down

If you need to keep your dog absolutely still and under control, nothing is more effective than the down command. If your dog is committed to a down-stay, he's not likely to get up. It's the most stable position in the dog-training universe. It's also the most difficult exercise for a small dog to learn.

Think about it a little, and it makes a lot of sense. Small dogs already feel vulnerable. They may be mighty carnivores in their minds, but their bodies look more like rabbits. Putting themselves in a down position, especially near other dogs, makes them extremely vulnerable. The only way they can do this exercise successfully is to completely trust you and to feel safe. That's why your patience and gentleness is especially important in this exercise.

Before you begin this exercise, the dog should be standing and relaxed. Most books and trainers will tell you to teach down from a sit. After years of trying this, my mentor, Ellie Wyckoff, told me to teach it from a stand. What an epiphany! Dogs who have recently learned to sit and stay are terribly confused when suddenly you're telling them to go down. If you start from a standing position, they're much less worried when learning this exercise.

- Hold a treat between your dog's front toes. He'll reach down for the treat and may drop into a down position. Say, "Good down!" and give him the treat.

- If he doesn't drop, keep the treat on the floor, pushing it slightly toward his chest. If he physically follows the treat with his nose, his chest will go down on the ground. Say, "Good down," and reward him when his chest rests on the ground.

Be patient. Sometimes it takes some maneuvering before your dog learns the down. If he's getting frustrated, reward partial success. So, if his chest is on the ground but his rear end is still high in the air, give him a treat with a "Yes!" for the partial success. Build on the partial success until he downs with his whole body, at which time say, "Good down" and treat him generously.

If It Doesn't Work

If you had a big dog, you could be assured that your dog would learn the down command if you held a cookie by his toes. While about 90 percent of small dogs will also learn down with this technique, the others won't. Why? Because their noses are already at ground level!

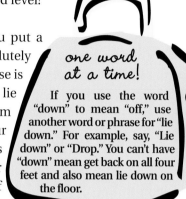

Dachshunds are a case in point. When you put a treat between a Dachshund's toes, he has absolutely no clue about what you want him to do. His nose is *already* at ground level—he doesn't need to lie down to get there. He has no idea you want him to lie down for him to get the treat from your hand. In honor of Dachshunds and other dogs who don't have to bend their legs to get their noses to the ground, here are two other ways of teaching your small dog to down.

one word at a time!

If you use the word "down" to mean "off," use another word or phrase for "lie down." For example, say, "Lie down" or "Drop." You can't have "down" mean get back on all four feet and also mean lie down on the floor.

Teaching Down on a Chair

The technique for teaching down on a chair or couch is exactly the same as the traditional technique outlined above, except you hold the treat a few inches below the level of the seat. The Dachshund or other short-legged breed has to bend his front legs to get to the treat, and in doing so, he's well on his way to learning down.

Be sure to set the dog up near the edge of the seat, or he won't be able to follow the treat with his nose over the end of the chair.

Be sure your dog is comfortable and understands "down" well on a chair before you try it on the ground. When he really understands it, you should be able to just say, "Down" on the ground, and he'll lie down.

The Dachshund Down

Most dogs learn "down" comfortably with the two methods outlined above. However, not every small dog is comfortable near the edge of a chair, and some seem to completely lose the memory of the treat once it's out of sight below the edge of the chair. For these dogs, we have a different way of teaching down. It's actually the first step in teaching the tricks "roll over" and "play dead."

With the dog standing, hold a treat next to his elbow. *Slowly* move the treat from the dog's elbow to his shoulder blade. Your dog will have to move his shoulders around to follow the treat and will lie down on his side. When he goes into the down position, tell him he's a very, very good dog and give him the treat.

With this technique, your dog will lie on his side instead of in the elegant Sphinx position. Don't worry about it. The important thing is to teach your dog a reliable down.

THE DOWN-STAY

Once your dog is comfortable doing a down, it's time to add the stay command. Teach this exactly the way you taught the sit-stay.

Introduce your dog to the down-stay gradually, ensuring he is comfortable with "down" before you advance to the next step.

After you tell your dog, "Down," take a step back about 6 inches and gently say, "Stay, good down-stay." Instantly, and while he is still in the down position, reward him. Just like the sit, he can't learn to down for one minute if he can't go down for one second.

When he succeeds at a one-second down-stay, expand the time to five seconds, ten seconds, etc. If he consistently gets up after (for example) 15 seconds, give him a 12-second stay and reward him. Help him succeed. Chain together two or more stays. Tell him, "Stay" and reward after 10 seconds, then step back and tell him, "Stay" and reward him after another 15 seconds.

Big Things to Remember About Training Small Dogs

If you practice the exercises in this section, you'll have a dog you can rely on and who trusts you and can rely on you. You'll feel so bonded that, as a friend of mine likes to say, you'll swear you gave birth to your dog. However, there are a few things to keep in mind to be sure that you're creating that bond and maintaining it.

keep it fun!

Remember, the down command is the most submissive position a dog can take. It makes your little dog feel extremely vulnerable to other dogs, to strangers, and even to you. Praise him, treat him, pet him, laugh, and smile. Let him know that this is a fun, enjoyable trick and that you're proud of him. All the encouragement will help him perform better and more reliably, and that might be the difference between life and death for your dog someday.

SAYING "NO" AND CORRECTIONS

Never, ever say "no" to or "correct" a dog who doesn't know the exercise. It will make him stop trying. You remember how hard it was when you were first learning how to read or do multiplication tables. Your dog has to work just as hard to learn sit and come. You wouldn't have liked school much if someone had yelled at you, "NO! The square root of 9 isn't 4. I can't believe how stupid and stubborn you are!"

If your dog makes a mistake, help him find the right answer by luring him into the exercise correctly.

If a dog absolutely knows something backward and forward, he still might make an honest mistake and forget. Remember, in normal learning, he will forget a command as it goes from his short-term to his long-term memory. Plus, dogs, like people, just have days they aren't as sharp as normal. Be as forgiving of your little dog as you expect him to be of you.

Telling your dog "no" shouldn't be unpleasant. There really are dogs who probably think their names are "No! No! Bad Dog!"—and that dog and human aren't having fun together. Rather than saying, "No!" to my dogs, I say, "Uh-uh." It's physically impossibly to say "uh-uh" in a mean voice. I think of "good" and "uh-uh" as being like "warmer" and "colder" in a guessing game. "Uh-uh" is a signal to my dogs that they're on the wrong track and should start again. It does not mean that I'm angry, disappointed, upset, or think that they're stupid. It merely gives them the information to figure out what I need from them.

"Uh-uh" is always followed by "good!" when the dog performs what I want. There is always at least one "good!" (and usually many more) for every one "uh-uh."

A SMALL DOG TRAINER'S RECIPE FOR SUCCESS

- Don't fall into the easy trap of becoming overly dependent on food rewards. When you are first teaching an exercise, food rewards are the easiest way to lure a dog into a position. But as soon as the dog has begun to understand the behavior, remember the reward should be variable and unpredictable. If you always give him a food reward, he will soon decide to only listen when you've got food in your pocket. Even a flat-faced Pekingese can tell whether or not you've got food. Instead, it's important that the dog doesn't know what the reward for doing the command will be, but he knows it will be something delightful!

- Don't ever try to compare your dog or your progress to anyone else's. Most especially, don't try to compare the dog you have now with some dog you had in the past. Every dog learns in his own way and at his own pace, and every dog can learn the exercises in this chapter! It's just like kids—all of them learn to talk, all of them learn to read. It doesn't matter who learns something first.

- Practice every day. Most of this you can practice on the spur of the moment, while you're watching TV, while you're playing with your dog, while you're getting the dog's breakfast. Practice is fun and happy—not grim! Don't stop practicing just because your dog "knows" the exercise. Dog brains have a lot in common with human brains, and they need to practice things to remember them clearly. Today, I couldn't sit down and do the most basic algebra problem, because I haven't practiced that skill in many, *many* years. If you want your dog to remember stay, come, and all the other basic commands, you need to practice them together regularly, even after he's mastered them.

Enjoy this time with your dog. The months and years pass all too quickly. Take the time to teach your dog his obedience, to tell him he's absolutely grand, and to savor the time you have together. You'll never get this day back that you could have spent deepening your relationship with the pint-sized dog with the heart as big as a mountain.

Finding a Safe Obedience Class for Your Small Dog

It can be fun and worthwhile to take a class with your dog. Dog training is a visual, 3-D activity, and especially if you want to do more advanced work with your dog, it helps to work with a capable trainer. Before considering taking a class or private lessons, check out the trainer. Here are some things to do:

- Talk with the trainer about her philosophy. Does she use modern, motivational methods? Does she believe in food rewards? If the answer is yes, then she might be a good trainer for a small dog. On the other hand, if she's an old-fashioned, jerk-and-pull trainer who thinks dogs should "do what I say or else," you and your dog aren't going to have a lot of fun.

- Ask the trainer what experience she's had training small dogs. Ideally, she's actually had a small dog of her own. Second best is someone who has worked with a lot of small dogs and can give you references.

- Go to her classes and see for yourself. Are the dogs and people having fun? Is the class under control or is it chaotic? Most important, do you think it's a place that's safe for your small dog? A class and instructor that might be perfectly fine for your neighbor's rowdy Labrador might be a disaster for your little Shih Tzu.

Often, a group class full of untrained, big dogs just isn't a safe place for your little dog. If you find an instructor whom you like, but you aren't comfortable with the beginner's class, talk with the instructor about some alternatives. Ask her to consider teaching a Small Dogs Only class. She might like the idea! I teach a Small Dog Class, and it's a trainer's slice of heaven. I'm not worried that any of these dogs is going to bite my arm off— a definite plus from a trainer's perspective! The dogs are fun, and the people who have these dogs are very attached and loving with them—factors that make it an enjoyable experience for the instructor. Plus, if no one else in the community is teaching a small dog class, it can be a nice marketing niche for the trainer.

Use this book (and any other training books you like) to train your dog well enough that the trainer will admit you into one of her more advanced classes. If the big dogs are well-trained, you don't have to be so worried.

Take private lessons. You'll have the trainer's expertise, but you won't have to worry so much about other dogs. Be sure that you practice in a variety of places, so your dog is exposed to different sights, sounds, smells, and people.

Remember, your small dog's safety is your primary responsibility. I like to say that other people might have bought their dogs for protection, but my dogs got me for their protection!

Pomeranian

Housetraining Your Small Dog

It's not your imagination. It really is harder to housetrain a small-breed dog. You may have reliably housetrained your Golden Retriever when he was eight weeks old; however, that's not likely to happen with your small breed dog. In fact, housetraining problems are the most common reasons that people return their dogs to the breeder or take them to a shelter. The question is: Why?

If you think about it, it's logical that small dogs are going to have more housetraining trouble than big dogs. Here are some of the reasons.

- **They have a difference sense of space.** A small dog might pee in the corner and feel proud of himself. In his mind, he's gone as far away from his bed as a full-sized dog who has gone to the far end of the yard. Lots of small dogs have trouble grasping the concept of distance.

- **They have smaller systems.** It can take a long time for systems to mature. Your puppy may be six months or older before his system is mature enough to hold back from urinating or defecating right after meals, exercise, or sleep. Expect to continue to work on the fundamentals of housetraining well into your puppy's adolescence.

- **Their genetics may be different.** Let's face it: If a Great Dane or Saint Bernard doesn't get the hang of housetraining pretty quickly, he's not likely to stay someone's pet for long. The odds are that dog will never, ever be bred. Because small accidents are much less difficult to live with, small dogs who have housetraining problems have reproduced for generations, probably since small companion dogs first appeared in medieval castles. Also, a toy dog may not have the same strong instinct to ask to be let out that a big dog has.

Don't worry! With a little patience and a lot of consistency and vigilance, your little dog can become reliably housetrained.

Step-by-Step Training

1. Confine your dog! It's not fair to expect your puppy to understand housetraining if you give him free run of the whole house (or the entire living room). He needs to be confined to a space he understands. Unless he's just pottied, keep him confined to a small area, such as your kitchen or bathroom. When you want him with you, tie a 6-foot leash to your waist so he doesn't have the room to make a mistake. (This also teaches him to hang out with you—a great lesson for a companion dog!) When you leave the house, confine the puppy to a crate, an exercise pen, or the corner of an indestructible room.

2.. Take your dog outside, don't just let him out the door. A small-sized puppy is likely to be lonely, or he may get distracted. He's not likely to potty on his own. Go out there with him, and praise, praise, praise when he potties.

3. Teach your puppy a "permission to potty" command. When he potties, say, "Good potty!" (or whatever word you choose) and reward him with petting and maybe even a treat. Eventually, when you say, "Potty!" your dog will potty. This saves enormous amounts of time in your life and is a real help when you're traveling and when you take your dog to unfamiliar surfaces.

4. Watch for your dog's signs that he needs to go out. Some dogs never get the idea of going to the door and asking to go out. They may come and look at you, circle around, or trot around restlessly. Learn to read your dog's way of telling you that he needs to potty.

Never punish your dog for a mistake. It only adds to your small dog's anxiety and slows down the process.

Think about your female's comfort. A tall clump of grass that a large dog would never notice is an insurmountable object to a toy-sized female when she tries to urinate. Take her to a part of the yard that doesn't have grass, such as a garden area. You might also have to shovel snow to give her a usable spot. Have faith! Housetraining your small dog can be a slow process, but one day the light will go on. Your dog can learn this!

When It's Not a Housetraining Problem

There are two situations in which otherwise well-housetrained dogs pee in the house: male territorial marking or leg lifting and submissive urination.

LEG LIFTING

Male toy dogs are notorious leg-lifters. They lift their legs and pee a small amount to mark territory. This is different from a dog who is pottying, which will

never snicker at someone else's problem

My dog, Pogo, came from an excellent Papillon breeder. He was raised in an extremely clean environment, and his mother is very reliably housetrained. This is the way that an easily housetrained dog starts life.

I work at home and have never had any trouble housetraining a dog. I knew housetraining Pogo would be a snap. I was (thankfully silently!) a little disdainful of anyone who couldn't easily housetrain a dog.

Pogo wasn't reliably housetrained until he was nine months old! My carpet never knew that he wasn't, because I took Pogo out every time he might need to potty. But I knew that he didn't know to ask to go outside and seemed sort of mildly surprised every time he pottied. We were outside trying to teach Pogo the concept so much the summer of his puppyhood that I had the best tan I've ever had in my life.

Every time Pogo pottied, I'd tell him, "Good potty!" and give him a treat, and I'd hand out treats to my other two dogs. I'd even give a treat to my cat, who was watching the whole thing through the screen door. As soon as Pogo would pee, the cat and both older dogs would get excited, knowing it was treat time. Pogo didn't have a clue.

Suddenly, one day, Pogo figured it out. It was almost like a light went on in his head that said, "Wow! I get it! You go outside and you potty! Cool!" He's been reliably housetrained since that day.

This taught me two lessons: 1) Small dogs are going to learn to be housetrained on their own timetable—all you can do is encourage them and manage around the problem; and 2) Never, ever snicker at anyone else's problems, for the universe has a way of teaching you its own lessons!

result in a noticeably larger amount of urine. A male dog can be otherwise perfectly housetrained, but still mark. This is particularly a problem in houses with multiple unneutered, male, toy-sized dogs.

Neutering your dog, especially when he's a puppy, is the best defense against territorial leg lifting. Rather than keeping an eagle eye on their dogs 24 hours a day, many people resort to putting belly bands (also called cummerbunds) on their male dogs. This is a strip of cloth that goes around the dog's tummy, lined with an absorbent pad to manage the problem.

my puppy ate what?!

It's disgusting to us humans, but often young puppies eat their own poop. If you have your dog on a well-balanced diet, this is probably just a habit and not a cause for alarm.

No one knows why some puppies eat poop. One explanation is that they're imitating (either consciously or instinctively) the cleaning-up that their mother does in the den.

It's a pretty easy habit to break, if you're consistent. Always go outside with your puppy at potty time. When he potties, tell him what a good, good puppy he is and have him follow you away from the waste. Later, go back and pick up the waste. (The theory is that this puppy shouldn't see you picking up waste, since he might decide he should pick up after himself in his own way.)

If he's a determined poop eater, put him on leash and lead him away from the scene. Don't scold him—you don't want him to think he isn't making you happy with his housetraining. The good news is that most dogs outgrow this gross habit by the time they're about six months old.

Submissive Urination

Many shy dogs will urinate when you pet them, greet them, or when they're excited. Submissive urination is a dog's way of telling you that he's no challenge to you; the dog is acknowledging in doggie terms that you're in charge.

Don't respond to submissive urination by yelling at the dog. Because these dogs are urinating to show they're submissive to you, they will only urinate more if you yell.

Instead, greet the dog with your hand under his chin, rather than over his head. The scariest greeting for any dog is for a hand to come over his head or back—the threat of this greeting is multiplied times ten if the dog is tiny.

Also, be very matter-of-fact when you come and go. Drama adds to the dog's need to urinate, so if you greet the dog slowly and casually, the dog will be less likely to turn on the flood. Place a washable mat at the front door, so if your dog does "leak" as he greets you, it's not a big deal. Just wash the mat.

Do the other exercises in this book to build your dog's confidence. Teach him obedience and practice gentle leadership techniques. As your dog gains confidence, his need to submissively urinate will be reduced and probably eliminated.

Indoor Solutions

Don't leave your small dog outside when you're not there to supervise, even if you have a securely fenced yard. It's too easy for your diminutive dog to scramble through a mouse-sized fence hole, dig underneath the gate, or hurt himself. That doesn't even begin to describe just how much danger he is in if someone is cruising the neighborhood to steal dogs; a small dog can bring big bucks among unscrupulous people.

If you can't be home often enough to give your dog a potty break, don't risk letting him run in and out through a doggie door. Instead, bring the outside in and create an indoor toilet system for your dog.

HOUSETRAINING PADS

Pet suppliers sell housetraining pads that can be a practical solution for indoor, small dogs over the long term. You place the pads, which have been treated with an odor that humans don't smell but that smells like urine to a dog, on the floor. Most dogs will pee and poop right on the pad.

These pads have absorbent material and plastic backing, kind of like a larger, thinner disposable baby diaper, so you can leave them on most floors without damaging the floor.

For best results, take your dog outside, use a potty command, encourage results, and reward accordingly.

Many people who live in condominiums, urban areas, or apartment buldings, or who must leave their dogs for longer periods of time, find these pads practical and convenient and use them during the entire lives of their small dogs.

LITTER BOXES

If you have a cat, he probably uses a litter box. If you have a dog who's sort of the size of a cat, he might do great with his own litter box.

Line a large-sized litter box (or larger short-sided plastic box of any kind) with an absorbent material. You can buy dog litter, or you can also experiment with cat litter—but be sure not to use clumping litter. If your dog swallows clumping litter, it forms into a solid mass in his tummy and might require emergency surgery if it gets caught in his digestive system. (Note: Don't let your cat and dog share the same litter box. Your dog might not mind, but your cat probably will. The last thing you want is a cat who won't use his litter box.)

GRASS BOXES

If you're a handy person (or know one), you can create a large, planter-type box of grass for your dog. This can be ideal for condo dwellers who have balconies. Your mini-dog will have a mini-lawn of his own. Even if you're not the Earth Mother type, you can purchase some sod to place in a large box. The sod will live with minimal care quite a while, and you can just replace it as needed.

TEACH "PERMISSION TO POTTY" INDOORS

Housetraining pads are treated with an attractive (to a dog) odor, so your dog will have a clue that it's okay to potty on that spot. To encourage your dog to potty in his litter box or grass box, place a little of his waste on the spot.

When you know that he needs to potty, take him over to his box or pad. Give him your permission to potty command. If he gets the idea, great. If not, keep taking him to this spot when he needs to eliminate, and keep telling him to "potty." When you leave your home, confine the dog in the same room with his box or pads. If he needs to potty in your absence, he's already been introduced to the system, and he's likely to use it when the need arises.

It's okay to take your dog outside sometimes for pottying and let him use his indoor system other times. After all, each is an area where he's had permission to potty.

Papillons

Solving Common Behavior Problems

The odds are if you have a small dog who's behaving badly, you have a worried dog. Growling, barking, snapping, showing teeth: All of these are behaviors of dogs who believe that they have to protect themselves. It must be pretty scary to be a 3-, 5-, or 10-pound dog who can't rely on the full-sized human in his life to protect him.

To help your worried dog, remember what we learned: 1) give your dog meals (don't free-feed him!); 2) have him sit (or do another trick) when you feed him or give him attention; 3) decide when and where he sleeps; and 4) tell him to wait at doors.

If you do these simple things, which won't add five minutes of time to your day, your dog will perceive you as his leader. He can take a deep breath and relax. He doesn't have to defend the house by himself; he can cooperate with the humans to do the job. He doesn't have to protect you from every relative or friend who wants to hug you, because he knows that you're competent to decide which people should touch you and which people shouldn't.

When you don't show leadership in a way that a dog can understand, he thinks that the head of his pack is incompetent. He will respond by either trying to take over or by becoming extremely worried. (If you've ever worked in a poorly run company, you've seen people behave in the same way.)

When you want to end problem behaviors, half the battle is simply letting the dog know, in non-violent doggie terms, that you're in charge. Do that, and many behavior problems will resolve themselves.

Taming the Armpit Piranha

Beware of the Armpit Piranha. You know what I mean: Those little dogs who seem to live in the crook of their doting human's arm, showing a full array of tiny

No Armpit Piranha here! This dog feels safe with these gentle children who are holding and petting him appropriately.

teeth when anyone dares to approach within 5 feet. (Thanks to Susan Fletcher, a terrific dog trainer in the Portland, Oregon area, who introduced me to this descriptive term!)

There are variations of the Armpit Piranha. For example, lots of small dogs don't like to share the bed, especially with the spouse of their favorite human. Sometimes it's a chair or a toy. In any event, the dog has decided that no one else is allowed to touch the person or object that he's claimed as his own. By taking control of the situation, you can reclaim your spouse, bed, and other valuables, and your dog will be a happier, calmer family member.

WHEN YOUR DOG WON'T LET PEOPLE NEAR YOU

Small dogs tend to define small territories, and nothing is easier to defend than a lap. Your devoted dog is likely to set up very clear boundaries that other people aren't allowed to cross. When they do, either by touching you or coming within a certain distance, your dog will let them know in a not-too-subtle way that they're supposed to back off. After all, he owns you. Right? Wrong!

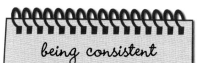

being consistent

If your dog is going to change his behavior, it's essential that you're absolutely consistent with your behavior. You can't allow him (and even laugh about it) to misbehave one day and then tell him "no" the next. Your dog will just learn to ignore you and view you as an unreliable person. Remember, dogs who are growling and snapping aren't happy. Your leadership in helping your dog change will improve the quality of his life and improve the bond that the two of you share.

You own you. If you merely put the dog on the ground when he gets nasty, he won't have a territory to defend. He'll stop growling and calm down. Meanwhile, let your dog know that you like people and want him to like people as well. The best way for him to decide that other people are good things is to have them feed him little treats. Carry treats with you on walks and ask people to feed the dog a little morsel. After he's used to accepting treats on the ground, progress to holding him and ask a friend to offer the treat.

If your dog is good, he gets the treat. If he growls or snarls, put him back on the floor and have your friend eat the treat. (Be sure to have something that humans like, because it's important for the friend to eat and swallow the treat!) Have your friend lick her lips and make a big deal about how wonderful the treat tasted. Wait a day or two and try again, first treating the dog on the ground and later sitting on your lap. If your

the dog who wouldn't let anyone leave

Pappy was a sweet-looking, 8-pound dog who ruled the roost. He wiggled happily when anyone arrived at the house. Unfortunately, he bit them when they tried to leave. Like a tiny version of the ogre who guards a bridge in a fairy tale, he decided that no one could go without his permission. The more you yelled at determined little Pappy, the more he snapped at your ankles.

Just an afternoon of working with Pappy had the problem well on its way toward being resolved. One brave friend agreed to be the person who came and went. When the friend said, "Good-bye!" the family members told Pappy, "Watch me!" and fed him treats. Within about three "Good-byes," the dog was turning to his family for a treat, leaving the friend unmolested. I left that session feeling like we'd accomplished a major breakthrough with the little dog—and we had. There was no reason to expect that dog to snap at anyone's ankles again.

A few months later, I ran into Pappy and his family and asked how his behavior was. He was back to biting everyone who had an ankle, they told me, chuckling.

I finally realized that, at some level, the family found it funny or flattering that little Pappy wouldn't let anyone leave. Of course, other days they were really upset, like when his little teeth snagged a pair of pantyhose or his antics made someone late for work or school.

This family could have changed Pappy's behavior any day. They just had to make a commitment to the change. You need to decide that you seriously want to change your dog's behavior, too, or the dog will go back to his same old habits.

friend continues to offer the dog a really yummy treat, sooner or later your pooch will figure out that it's better to be a good boy than to miss out on such a delicacy.

If your dog reverts to snarling, just say to him, "Oops! Too bad! You've lost your lap privileges!" and put him gently on the floor. That's it—no elaborate discussions, no yelling, no wailing. Your dog will learn that good behavior allows him to be on your lap and maybe even earns him a treat. Bad behavior gets him placed on the floor and all the fun is gone. Over time, he'll make the right choice.

RECLAIMING YOUR BED

It's amazing how much trouble one little dog can cause in a king-sized bed. If your dog is growling at your spouse when he comes into the bedroom, growling when you move in bed, or otherwise making sleep a nightmare, you need to work with him.

Overall, I have no objections to dogs in the bed. My three sleep with me, and I consider that a luxury. The key to a harmonious bedroom is for the dog to understand it's your bed, and he has the privilege of sleeping there. (Remember, in doggie terms, the lead dog decides who sleeps where, and when.)

Teach your dog "on" and "off." Teach your dog that you decide when he's on the bed or other furniture. Tell him, "On" and encourage him to come up on the bed. Tell him he's a good boy. Then say, "Off!" and reward him for jumping off. Play the "on" and "off" game regularly to reinforce the fact that you decide, not the dog, when he's on the bed.

Have a reasonable alternative for when your dog isn't behaving. If you have a dog who is territorial about his bed or who has been growling or snapping any place, any time during the day, he shouldn't sleep on your bed that night. Be prepared with a reasonable alternative. Have a nice, comfy crate set up next to the bed. It should be a nice place to sleep, lined with soft bedding. It's fine to have toys in the crate, as well.

When your dog growls, scoop him up and unemotionally put him in the crate. When my dog, Pogo, was a pushy adolescent, twice he growled at one of the other dogs on the bed. I was prepared for this, since I knew Pogo was in a phase where he was trying out his boundaries. I had the crate by the bed and just calmly said, "Dogs in my bed don't growl," and put him in the crate. After the second time, he never growled at the other dogs in bed again, because he knew it would lower his status, not increase it, to behave that way.

If your dog whines in the crate, ignore him. He's in a nice, comfy spot. He's in the same room with you, so he knows he's safe and part of the pack. He's just lost the privilege of being on your bed. He can earn the privilege back tomorrow, but tonight he stays put.

TOY POSSESSION

Many dogs are highly possessive of bones or toys. It can be scary to see your sweet little baboo turn into a snarling beast who won't let you near him. It feels like a scene from *The Exorcist*.

The best solution is to teach your dog that it's not in his best interest to be territorial with his toys. It's easiest to deal with this problem when the dog is a puppy, but the same techniques can also be applied to an adult dog.

Avoid toy possessiveness by teaching your dog from puppyhood to trade one toy for another.

- Give and Take and Give Toys: Make giving a toy a game. Give the toy to the dog, then take it, and then immediately give it back. Laugh when you do it. Your dog learns having a toy is not a big deal, since he can expect it back.

- Teach Trade: Give your dog a low-value toy, something that isn't one of his favorites. Then hold a very high-value treat (such as a piece of steak) and say, "Trade!" Almost always, the dog will be thrilled to trade the low-value toy for the high-value treat. After you've done the trade, you can give the dog his original toy back.

When you play "trade," always make sure you have something in your hand that the dog prefers to whatever he has in his paws. (If he doesn't want to trade, you can just walk away, or better yet, you can eat his high-value treat in front of him so he knows that he made the wrong choice by not trading.) Over time, your dog will learn that "trade" is a great game, and he doesn't need to horde anything.

use it (nicely) or lose it

If there's just one thing that makes your dog extremely possessive, consider eliminating it from his routine. If the only thing that he growls over is a certain toy, get rid of the toy or only allow him to play with it at certain times.

Almost every puppy goes through the "keep away" phase where he steals something—inevitably something that's dangerous for a puppy—and runs around the house, seemingly laughing at you because you're too slow to catch him.

"Trade" is the best response to this not-so-funny game. If your dog knows that "Trade!" means that he'll be getting the yummiest treat in the household, he's likely to swap whatever evil thing he's got in his mouth for your first-class treat.

It's important that you always give the dog the best deal in the trade—you want him to come to you no matter what. He won't willingly give up the "toy" if he doesn't think he's going to get something great in exchange.

Dog Aggression

A friend of mine who works in an emergency veterinary hospital ran into me one day. She had a small dog, and I'd carped to her about the importance of not letting her tiny dog challenge big dogs.

"There are four small dogs at the hospital this week," she reported to me. "All of them were attacked by big dogs." At least one of those dogs died as a result of his wounds.

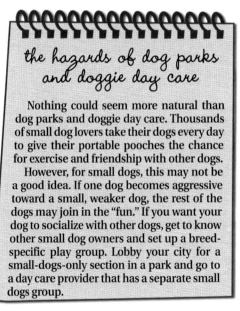

the hazards of dog parks and doggie day care

Nothing could seem more natural than dog parks and doggie day care. Thousands of small dog lovers take their dogs every day to give their portable pooches the chance for exercise and friendship with other dogs.

However, for small dogs, this may not be a good idea. If one dog becomes aggressive toward a small, weaker dog, the rest of the dogs may join in the "fun." If you want your dog to socialize with other dogs, get to know other small dog owners and set up a breed-specific play group. Lobby your city for a small-dogs-only section in a park and go to a day care provider that has a separate small dogs group.

If your little dog growls and snarls at a big dog, the big dog is likely to respond with a bite. That's life among dogs. If a big dog bites another large dog, the dogs seldom seriously hurt each other. The dogs might require some stitches, but more often than not, no permanent damage is done. At the end of the altercation, they might even be friends.

That's not what happens with little dogs. The bite that would leave a small wound on a Labrador will crush your Yorkie's ribs. The nip at the nape of the neck that wouldn't penetrate a Collie's fur will end up in a deathly shake that will snap the neck of a Chihuahua. If your dog challenges the big dog, it's your fault if the big dog responds like a dog and hurts him.

RULES TO LIVE (LONG) BY

- Don't allow your small dog to have prolonged eye contact with, growl at, or snarl at other dogs. Not ever. Period. Teach your dog to look at you (remember that old stand-by of "watch me!") when a larger dog comes by, so your dog can't establish eye contact or get in trouble.

- If your dog is likely to be aggressive with another dog, prevent any possible contact. When you see a dog coming, pick your dog up, and put him on the side of your body where the other dog won't see him and he can't see the other dog.

- Don't ever think it's okay that your dog is yapping, snapping, and snarling at another dog. This isn't a small dog acting like a big dog; it's a small dog acting like he's challenging other dogs, and one of them is likely to react. If you secretly admire this trait in your little dog, get over it, especially if you want him to live a long life.

ROUGH PLAY

Every time I see a really small dog roughhousing with a big one, I cringe. Inevitably, the people who love the dogs say, "Isn't it great? They love to play together. The little guy dishes out more than the big one."

What I see is a recipe for disaster. Watch how really small dogs play with really big ones. They're very aggressive and tense. The dog is darting in and out. It's highly possible that the game will quickly turn into a quarrel, and the small dog always, always, always loses the quarrel. In addition, playing so roughly with big dogs makes the dog a poor candidate for playing with dogs his own size. These dogs are so used to overly aggressive play that they don't know how to play politely. Limit your contact to other small breeds or very gentle, calm, larger dogs for your small dog's safety.

Excessive Barking

People who aren't overly fond of our lap-sized dogs often call them "yap dogs." They sometimes have a point. Many small dogs, to put it kindly, are "verbally gifted." In fact, most small-breed dogs bark noticeably more, than their larger counterparts. Their constant barking can grate on your nerves, like the sound of fingernails on a chalkboard. There are several reasons that small dogs tend to be barkers.

- Humans are more forgiving of barking in a small dog. Often they don't even seem to notice that their dogs are barking; they just talk louder to be heard over the din. If this had been a full-sized dog, the same person wouldn't put up with the noise.

- Small dogs are more worried than big dogs. When a little dog is barking non-stop, people will often say with a note of pride, "He sure thinks he's a big dog." Nothing could be farther from the truth. Non-stop barking is often a sign that the dog is insecure, and he figures that the best defense is a good offense. So he's trying to sound big, brave, and tough to feel safe. The tips that help you become the leader in your relationship also help with barking problems. When your dog knows that you are the leader, it will help reduce his anxiety, and he will likely bark less once he's calmer.

- Small dogs are bored. All dogs need physical and mental stimulation. Too often, small dogs are treated more like stuffed animals than live ones. They quickly learn that barking gets attention, even if it's negative attention. In a dog's life, negative attention is better than being bored. So your dog will bark; you'll say, "Stop it!" The dog realizes it works, so he barks again; you'll say, "Stop it!" And on it goes.

With some time and attention, you can bring this problem under control. Here's what to do:

- **Acknowledge what your dog is telling you.** Dogs know they hear things we don't. Like any sensible watchdog, your dog will want to tell you what's going on. If you ignore your dog or just tell him to be quiet, he may decide that you don't understand his message. He's likely to bark louder and more insistently. Instead of yelling at him to shut up, acknowledge what he's telling you. Go with him to the window and say, "I see the cat; thanks for letting me know." This will usually end the cycle, because your dog will know that you heard what he had to say.

- **Teach him to whisper.** Your little dog can't bark unless he breathes in first. As he's taking that breath, say, "Good whisper!" and give him a treat if one's handy. Within minutes, your pocket-sized pooch will be coming up to you doing silent barks to get your attention. Silent barks are good; noisy barks are incredibly irritating. Reward the silent barks.

- **Take away his chance to react.** I must admit that my dog, Pogo, is a squirrel addict. Pogo (appropriately named!) would bounce up and down and scream while he watched squirrels scurrying along the top of the backyard fence. For a while, I had a 4-foot-high line of nose prints across my sliding glass door, an impressive accomplishment for a 12-inch-tall dog.

The solution was to convince Pogo that he was better off watching the squirrels quietly than making such a racket. When Pogo would start screaming and screeching, I'd just pick him up and hold him on my lap someplace where he couldn't see out the window. Pogo quickly learned that acting like a lunatic only took him farther from the squirrel. He learned to control his behavior in order to keep the squirrel in sight. Now, he will whine a little, but that's acceptable to me.

- **Give your dog a job.** Bored dogs are noisy dogs. They bark at leaves in the wind, the sound of butterfly wings, the breathing of a cat down the street. Your noisy dog may just need something fun to do. Go for a walk, take an obedience or agility class, or teach your dog tricks. Ask your dog to pick up and put away his own toys. A friend of mine (with full-sized, busy dogs) calls herself an amusement park on two legs. Be the same for your little dog.

Pogo is a competitive obedience dog and is a certified therapy dog who visits kids regularly in a local hospital. I don't mind asking him to control himself around squirrels, because I know he has plenty of other outlets for all his energy.

GOOD BARKING

I'd recently moved into a new house in a nice neighborhood. It was late on a Saturday night when suddenly, my three little dogs started barking extremely loudly. They ran into my writing room, growling and making a fuss. I figured that someone was out on the lawn, so I turned the lights on and off, letting any prowler know I was home. A few minutes later, the dogs went running into the bedroom, barking again. I turned on the light in that room, too.

It wasn't until the next day that I saw that the screen had been removed from my writing room window, which was fortunately closed. A big handprint was on the window, where the intruder tried to open it. The screen was halfway off of my bedroom window, which had been open.

debarking surgery

You may have heard about debarking surgery, which reduces your dog's bark to a whisper. Please think twice and then think again before considering this for your dog.

Debarking surgery cuts the dog's vocal chords. Not only does this end barking, but it also makes it impossible for the dog to growl or whine. When you've debarked a dog, you've just eliminated much of his ability to communicate with people and with other dogs. My dog, Goldie, was debarked before I got her. When other dogs get in her face, she snaps at them, because she can't warn them away with a little growl.

Goldie, unfortunately, has some paralysis in her neck, where the veterinarian who performed the surgery apparently nicked a nerve. We watch carefully to make sure that this paralysis isn't causing her to have difficulty swallowing, which could be lethal.

If your dog has an issue with barking, please train your pooch—don't try to solve the issue with surgery.

I called the police to make a report. The officer told me that there had been a lot of recent break-ins in the area and that the barking of my dogs and my light flickering had undoubtedly saved me from finding a burglar in my home. The officer said that I had great dogs who did exactly what dogs are supposed to do. His only recommendation for what I should have done differently: I should call 911 the next time my dogs bark, because they know what they're doing!

The lesson is that not all barking is bad. My dogs knew something was wrong, and told the intruder and told me. My three dogs weigh in at 6, 8, and 10 pounds, but they're big-time heroes to me.

Door Dashing

Small dogs can be adventurous, and some of those little legs can fly across the ground faster than any human can follow. Too many small dogs dash through doors. This can be deadly; once out of the house, even a careful driver might not see your little dog until it's too late. I personally know of two toy dogs that dashed through doors and never returned to their worried families. Don't trust your dog near an open door, especially if he's new to your home. A combination of training and vigilance is your best defense against this worrisome habit.

- With your dog's leash on, practice "wait" at your doorway. Open the door, say, "Wait," and give the dog a treat. Reinforce the wait command every time you go outside, so at least your dog will hesitate before he thinks of crossing a threshold.

- Practice the come command from the outside in. With your dog on a leash, have him outside, and you inside the open door. Call to him, and when he comes back inside, give him big treats and praise. This shows him that it's great to come inside when you're inside.

- Manage the front door. Keep a baby gate across your entrance hall. Don't give your dog the chance to dash through the door. Don't ever, ever trust him around open doors, not for a minute.

Separation Anxiety

Separation anxiety is a serious but fairly rare disorder. Dogs who experience true separation anxiety are experiencing something like a panic attack. They become so terrified that they drool copious amounts and are so frantic that they'll break their teeth or even a bone trying to get out of their confining pen.

If your dog has honest-to-goodness separation anxiety, ask your veterinarian for help and preferably a referral to a board-certified veterinary behaviorist. These veterinarians are the canine equivalent of psychiatrists and can tailor a treatment program of behavior modification and possibly some short-term use of calming medications to help your dog. Dogs that are diagnosed with separation anxiety have to learn to be 2 inches, 2 feet, and 2 rooms away from the people they love. Until they learn that, they shouldn't be left alone.

While clinically defined separation anxiety isn't common, it's extremely common for small dogs to decide they don't like being left alone and to let you know it. Think of this from your dog's perspective. Small dogs typically spend more hours with their human family than other dogs by far. A dog who is with his humans this much naturally isn't going to like the idea of being left alone. Still, he needs to learn that he's perfectly safe when you leave him and that you'll come back soon.

Teaching Your Dog to be Alone

- **If you've never left him alone, start training for it now.** Don't wait for the big emergency when you're distraught and he'll be confined for hours at a time. Practice leaving him three minutes, five minutes, ten minutes, etc.—working gradually to leaving him for a few hours at a time.

- **Make coming and going matter-of-fact.** You don't get dramatic when you leave a human relative; don't get dramatic with your dog. If you do, he'll be convinced that something must be very wrong.

- **Leave him in a manageable space.** He'll feel more comfortable if he's in a confined space. I like exercise pens (little portable fences you can easily put up and down in your home) better than crates, because the dogs have a little more space, but your dog might prefer a crate. The Nylabone® Fold-Away Pet Carrier is perfect for smaller dogs. Don't give him the run of the whole house, because then he has to worry about the whole house.

Your small dog may feel safer in a crate.

- **Leave him with interactive toys.** Purchase puzzle toys that dispense kibble when your dog shakes or moves them. Rhinos are chew toys that you fill with treats (such as cheese, peanut butter, and kibble) to keep the dog busy. Choose small sizes for small dogs.

- **Tell him that you're leaving.** When I leave, I always say, "I'll be back. Radar's in charge when I'm gone!" The dogs have their toys, and they settle down to enjoy the rest. (If I'm just running outside to grab the paper or the mail, I always say, "I'll be right back!" so they know it's not a long wait.)

- **When you return, be pleasant but not wildly emotional.** You just came back from the store, not the space shuttle. Don't convey to your dog that it's so dangerous out there that you're relieved to come home.

when our worries affect our dogs

I have a good friend who got a Papillon when her old dog was very elderly and sick. She grieved enormously when the old dog died, but found a lot of comfort in the new, young adult dog who had come into her home. The only problem was that the young dog had "abandonment issues." She didn't even like it when my friend left the room.

When I talked with my friend about it, I realized that she was terrified at the thought of her new dog dying some day, because it was so painful to lose her old one. Unfortunately, she was communicating that to her healthy, young, otherwise very happy dog. Who knows if animals have a clear telepathic bond with us or if they just sense our emotions? In any event, this dog was picking up on my friend's fear that they would be separated, so even a few seconds of separation worried the Papillon enormously.

Over time, my friend's grief over the loss of her old dog became less immediate, and she made a conscious effort to convince the Papillon (and herself) that nothing bad was about to happen. As a result, the Papillon is much more relaxed and confident, whether or not my friend is in the room with her. That confidence has improved the quality of the dog's life markedly.

- **If you return home to a housetraining accident or destroyed property, don't get upset.** It was your lack of planning that created the conditions that allowed this to happen. The dog won't know why you're so angry when you come home and will just be more anxious next time (and therefore more likely to engage in anxious behavior).

- **Relax!** Compared to other dogs, your dog probably lives in Doggie Disneyland. Don't feel guilty about leaving your dog alone for reasonable periods of time.

Little Commands That Solve Lots of Problems

The real value of training is having a day-to-day relationship with your dog. Sometimes it's the small things that make a difference. Here are three handy commands that will make life much easier for your small dog and for you.

TEACHING "LEAVE IT!"

It's a long distance from the head of a Great Dane to the ground. There's some chance that you'll be able to grab his mouth or the object he has put in his mouth before he can swallow something he finds on the sidewalk. There's no way you can react quickly enough to stop a small dog from appropriating what's on the ground for himself. After all, his nose is already there. Instead, teach "Leave it!" so when you see him mouthing someting you can stop his action.

- Put a low-value toy on the ground—something that doesn't thrill him. Have a high-value, yummy treat in your hand.

- Walk your dog on a leash in the vicinity of the toy. Make sure he sees the toy, then show him the treat. When he grabs the treat from your hand, say, "Good leave it!" Cheer for his wise choice.

- Repeat this process several times, treating and cheering for his choices. When he's learned "leave it," he'll happily abandon what he sees.

TEACHING "CHECK IT OUT"

While most troubles come from dogs trying to grab things they shouldn't, a lot of problems can also arise when dogs are scared of simple things, such as a scrap of paper, a stuffed animal, or a broom. Because our dogs are little, even small objects can loom ominously above them, making them worry. You can erase many of your dog's worries by teaching him "Check it Out."

fall down and go boom

Life isn't always predictable; sometimes little accidents happen, such as when something falls near your dog or on your dog. If he's not seriously hurt, don't make him think it's a major catastrophe, or he'll become a worried little dog. So, when I drop the silverware on the kitchen floor and it startles my dog, or one of my dogs falls into a tidepool at the beach, I don't say, "Oh you poor, sweet, sad darling! That is so terrible!" Instead, I laugh and say, "Wow! That was silly, wasn't it?" They shake themselves off and go happily on their ways.

It's a lot like the mom who makes a huge production of her toddler falling over versus the one who says, "You fall down and go boom!" The child with the hysterical mother becomes worried about walking and other new experiences, while the child with the relaxed mom laughs and gets up and walks some more.

- Start with an object your dog doesn't find scary, such as a handkerchief. Put it on the floor, and hold a treat next to it. Say, "Check it out!" and let the dog go up and take the treat. While he's there, show him how much fun the handkerchief is.

- Hide the treat under the handkerchief and say, "Check it out!" Your dog will have a great time finding the loot and will decide this is a fun game. Play this game with several objects that aren't scary: little paper cups, your purse, a piece of paper. The dog is rewarded sometimes with food, sometimes with the joy of playing with this fun object.

- When you encounter something that makes the dog a little worried, say, "Check it out!" When he sniffs it, cheer, laugh, and clap. He'll learn that it's fun to check out new things, especially when you say it's okay.

When rewarding your dog for a job well done, encourage him to gently take the treat from your hand.

TAKING A TREAT NICELY

While not all rewards in dog training should be food rewards, they're the handiest to use, especially when a dog is first learning an exercise. The whole premise sort of falls apart if you feel your life is in danger every time "Jaws" reaches to grab for his treat. It's also worrisome to have a dog who might leave toothprints on a small child who's holding a cookie.

Happily, this problem is easily remedied with most dogs. Hold a treat firmly in your fist. I know—this seems like you're just offering your hand as hamburger to your pushy dog. I don't know why it works, but it does. Your dog won't bite your hand. (Another pleasure of small dogs is that their teeth are probably too small to eat your whole fist.) Soon, he'll reach his tongue out to get the treat. When he's delicately reaching out his tongue, say, "Good treat!" and let him have the food morsel. Repeat this process over time, until he gently takes treats from your hand.

Chinese Crested

Training Your Small Dog for the Real World

Coping With the Veterinarian

The most important hour your dog spends every year is at his annual checkup with his veterinarian. This is the time when your dog's doctor can discover cancer in the early stages, diagnose heart problems that can be treated, and generally help your dog live for many long, happy years. Sadly, if your dog is wriggling, squirming, snarling, and snapping, your veterinarian can't do his or her job. One vet put it to me this way, "It's like taking your car to a mechanic and telling him that something is wrong with the car and he needs to fix it, but he can't touch the car."

PRACTICE TOUCHING

Review the previous chapters and practice touching your dog all over his body, giving him names for his body parts. One of the biggest problems at the veterinarian's office is that many dogs don't want anyone looking at their teeth or inside their mouths. Make sure that touching your dog's muzzle and lips is part of his regular routine. As he learns to be comfortable with the mouth area, practice pulling up his lips and looking at his front teeth. The more you can practice gently opening your dog's mouth, the better prepared your dog will be to accept potentially life-saving medical treatment. (As you acclimate your dog to having his mouth handled, mentally compare the size of your dog's teeth with the jaws of a big breed and silently thank your lucky stars that you love little dogs!)

You can also prepare your dog to deal with a stethoscope. This contraption is very scary to a dog who doesn't see one regularly. Touch your dog with a variety of objects—plastic bags, spoons, crinkled up aluminum foil—so it isn't upsetting to him to feel the cold metal and plastic of the stethoscope.

MAKE THE VET'S OFFICE FUN

Take your dog to the veterinarian's, feed him cookies, and go home. If someone in a white coat is available, ask that person to give the dog some treats, too. As your dog gets comfortable in the vet's office, ask your pooch to "sit" and "down," and reward him for his good behavior. Basic obedience—sit, stay, down—helps your veterinarian tremendously.

Make appointments fun, too. Bring your dog's favorite treat and give him his cookies while your veterinarian is examining him. (Of course, check with your veterinarian that treats are appropriate; for example, it's important that food is withheld prior to your dog having surgery, even a simple teeth cleaning.)

I learned the power of treats at the vet's office from a very progressive veterinarian where I used to take my animals. The front desk staff, the vet techs, and the veterinarians would all offer the dogs treats. After a few visits, the dogs would start yipping with joy when we got near the vet's office. They loved that place because the fun of getting continuous cookies outweighed the few moments of unpleasantness of shots, temperature taking, and other necessary procedures. (In fact, I'm thinking I wouldn't mind going to my own doctor as much if he'd give me a hot fudge sundae after he examined me.)

Regular trips to the veterinarian are a must for your pet; use treats to make these visits a positive experience for him.

PLAN AHEAD

Can you imagine what it must be like to be a veterinarian and have a dog suddenly lunge and bite? Now imagine how upset you would be if the person with the dog said, "Oh, he does that!"

Even though your dog is small, his bite can still hurt and even injure his veterinarian and veterinary staff. Be respectful of the hard job that veterinarians perform. If your dog might bite, let the veterinary staff know ahead of time so they can deal with the situation.

If your dog needs to be muzzled, practice using a muzzle at home so it won't add to the dog's stress.

If you follow the advice throughout this book about providing leadership, acclimating your dog to touch, and giving your dog basic training, the chances are good that he'll learn to relax at the veterinarian's office and he'll turn into a model patient.

CHRONIC PROBLEMS

Some dogs have chronic problems that require regular medical checkups. Be sure to acclimate the dog to being touched on those sensitive areas. At the same time, be sure not to *only* be touching that part of his body, or he'll begin to worry about it.

So, if your dog has a paw that needs some sort of regular attention, check his paw (and say, "Good foot!" when you do!), then check out his ears, his tail, or his teeth. Handling a problem area should be routine and comfortable for your dog— not scary.

GIVING MEDICINE

One of the struggles that every dog lover faces is giving his or her dog medicine. This is usually a much bigger problem with small breeds than large. If you have a Labrador Retriever, you can slip an enormous pill in a hot dog, and your Lab is likely to swallow the whole thing, licking his lips in appreciation. On the other hand, if you have a small-breed dog, the chances are that he'll notice a pill the size of a grain of sand in even the finest liver pâté.

a tale of two papillons

I'd taken Radar, my Papillon, to the veterinarian's to get his teeth cleaned. He was a model patient. Although you could see from his eyes that he was a little worried, he calmly accepted the poking and prodding and wagged his plumed tail to thank the veterinarian and technicians for their gentle handling.

"Is this a normal temperament for a Papillon?" asked the veterinarian.

"Radar is a very good boy, but they should all be like he is, friendly and compliant," I answered.

"Well, we had one in yesterday who wasn't like this at all," said the vet. "She was trying to bite us. Her name was Angel."

There are two lessons in this story: The first is to be sure to touch your dog so that he feels comfortable and confident everywhere he goes. The second is think twice before you name your dog Angel—you're just asking for trouble!

You can always try hiding pills in your dog's food. The danger is that a sick dog will become very suspicious of what you're feeding him when he finds a pill in his food. Some sick dogs that already weren't eating well have actually stopped eating because they became leery of the food. So, if you have a finicky pooch, or if you're going to need to give your dog medication over a long period of time, teach him the word "medicine."

Calmly hold your dog, while you have a favorite yummy treat on hand. You might want to show the dog that you have the yummy treat waiting for him. Say, "Medicine," and quickly and efficiently give him the pill or liquid medication. Even if he squirms and wiggles, tell him, "Good medicine!" and instantly give the treat.

If you do this consistently for your dog, he'll learn to stand quietly and calmly to take even distasteful medication, then wag his tail, waiting for his reward. It's like the song from *Mary Poppins* says: A spoonful of sugar does help the medicine go down.

PILL PROBLEMS

It can be hard to get a small dog to swallow a big pill. If you're having trouble getting pills down your dog's throat, ask your veterinarian if there is a liquid form of the medicine. If you have a small dog, it's easy to hold him with one hand and insert the liquid medicine through a syringe with the other.

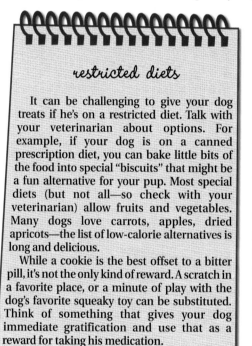

restricted diets

It can be challenging to give your dog treats if he's on a restricted diet. Talk with your veterinarian about options. For example, if your dog is on a canned prescription diet, you can bake little bits of the food into special "biscuits" that might be a fun alternative for your pup. Most special diets (but not all—so check with your veterinarian) allow fruits and vegetables. Many dogs love carrots, apples, dried apricots—the list of low-calorie alternatives is long and delicious.

While a cookie is the best offset to a bitter pill, it's not the only kind of reward. A scratch in a favorite place, or a minute of play with the dog's favorite squeaky toy can be substituted. Think of something that gives your dog immediate gratification and use that as a reward for taking his medication.

If the veterinarian prescribes medication that requires large-sized pills or large amounts of liquid medication, ask him or her if there is an effective prescription that might fit better for a dog with a tummy the size of a golf ball.

Grooming Challenges

Many small dogs require regular trips to the groomer. Cute, little, and fluffy seem to apply to many smaller breeds. Some breeds, such as Maltese, Poodles, Shih Tzu, and Yorkies, require professional groomers or very dedicated caregivers. Other small dogs may find themselves at the groomer every now and then for a day at the "spa."

If you have a dog who doesn't like to go to the groomer, prepare him for the experience in much the same way you prepared him to go to the veterinarian's. Get him used to being touched all over, especially the paws. Take him to the groomer's and have the groomer give him treats, then take him home.

The best gift you can give your dog is to keep him regularly combed and brushed between trips to the groomer. Mats are incredibly painful for your pooch. As they tangle with each other, they pull your dog's skin. Dogs with lots of mats are in pain all the time, and just walking or sitting can be excruciating.

If you have a long-haired dog, brush him every day. Go down to the skin; don't just groom the hair that's on top of the mats. Follow the brushing by gently pulling a comb through your dog's coat. As always, give your dog treats and praise as you groom him, and he'll think the whole process is pretty cool. The trip to the groomer will become the doggie equivalent of a trip to Disneyland!

NAIL TRIMMING

Keeping your dog's nails trimmed is one of the most important things you can do for his comfort and for his health. Long nails make every single step your dog takes uncomfortable for him. If you can hear his nails clicking on the floor, you're hearing the sound of discomfort and even pain. With small dogs, it only takes an extra quarter inch of nail to push your dog's feet out of alignment. Over the years, the structure

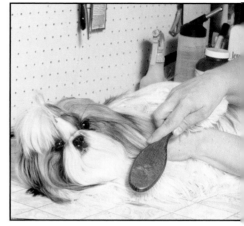

If you are unable to find the time necessary to groom your dog, a professional groomer may be the perfect solution.

of his paw and pastern will grow more exaggerated, resulting in pain, arthritis, and possibly even deformity.

All of this is completely preventable with regular nail clipping. Unfortunately, that's easier said than done. Many (even most) dogs hate to have their nails trimmed. They'll pull and squirm, growl, or wriggle. It's easy to give up. Instead of giving up, train your dog.

- Touch his feet every day. If he's relaxed when you touch them, massage his feet. Rub the space between the toes. Make touching a fun experience for him. Don't make this a battle of wills. One of the great advantages of small dogs is that they fit on our laps. Hold your dog on your lap and grab a paw. If your dog tries to pull the paw away, don't fight him, but don't let go. Just hold on gently and let him move his foot wherever he wants. Amazingly quickly, he'll give up fighting about possession of his paw.

Make nail trimming quick and painless for your dog by gradually introducing him to the process.

- Change your dog's view of nail clippers from negative to positive. Touch your dog's paw with the toenail clipper, give him a treat, then call it a day. The next day, touch his paw with the clipper and squeeze the clipper near the dog's foot, so that he hears the noise of nail clipping. Reward him by treating him. Keep the association with nail clippers pleasant in your dog's mind as you spend time each day with the dog, the nail clippers, and treats.

- After your dog is relaxed around the nail clippers, clip one nail, being careful to just trim the very tip. Give him a big treat and tell him he's good. That's enough for the first day. The next day, trim two nails. Continue to give your dog plenty of treats and praise. He may never love having his nails done, but he's very likely to relax while you do this necessary chore.

- The most important way to help your dog relax is for you to relax! You aren't going to amputate your dog's leg; you're trimming his toenails. Don't be tense, upset, or irritable, or your dog will pick up on it. (Imagine going to a manicurist who said, "Oh dear! I'm not sure I can do this! What if I hurt you?! Ohmygod what if you bleeeeed??!!" That's what it feels like to your dog when you're nervous.) Take a deep breath, relax, and competently trim his nails. You can do this!

the right equipment

The world belongs to people with the right tools, and nail trimming is no exception. Use the smallest, sharpest nail trimmers you can find for your dog. Your dog will be more comfortable, and you'll be more precise and confident.

You can use cat toenail clippers for toy-sized dogs. These operate like little scissors and are easy to manipulate. It's easy to take just a tiny bit of nail off with these, because they're quite easy to control.

Be sure your nail clippers are sharp. If they're dull, they'll squeeze your dog's toenails, which is very uncomfortable. If your nail trimmers seem dull, get a new pair. They aren't very expensive, and your dog will appreciate it.

Happy Travelers

For dog lovers, nothing defines the good life more than a road trip with our dogs. A trip to the beach, a hike around a mountain lake, even a day with the relatives: It's all more fun when you're in the company of your dog. Of course, the trip isn't any fun for any of you if your dog gets carsick. If you've been reading this book carefully so far, you probably know the answer to carsickness: Help your dog view travel as a happy experience, not a scary one!

Start out by just hanging out near your car, letting your dog "help" you unload groceries or wash the car. Put him in the car for just a moment and let him out. Work up to driving around the block, and then go for short trips to enjoyable places, such as a local park.

Remember to make sure that trips usually end up someplace fun, not just the veterinarian's office. If every time you got in the car someone took you to the doctor to be poked and prodded, you'd probably develop an aversion to cars, too.

Experiment with ways to make your carsick dog more comfortable. If he's throwing up with the crate at the back of your car, move it to the floor of the front seat (where the airbag can't reach it). If he's upchucking in the front, try the middle seat. Try experimenting with different crates—the Nylabone® Fold-Away Pet Carrier is safe for traveling. Keep the windows open for air circulation. Some dogs do better when they can see out the window; others do worse, so try different positions with the crate. If your dog's carsickness is severe, talk with your veterinarian about whether medication might help.

A crate, such as the Nylabone® Fold-Away Pet Carrier, is perfect for traveling and folds away for easy storage.

AIRPLANE RIDES

Most small dogs will fit into a soft-sided dog carrier that you can bring on a flight as carry-on luggage. If you've crate trained your dog and have introduced him to his airline carrier, he'll acclimate to going on a plane just as he learned to ride in a car. Lots of small dogs are frequent flyers, and time spent with you in the cabin is much less traumatic and less potentially dangerous than going by cargo.

Airplane travel can be scary and occasionally dangerous. Most dogs are required to travel in the cargo hold. There are rare but sad situations in which the hold wasn't properly heated, a dog didn't make a connection and was left without proper care, or a dog escaped from airport employees and ran away.

Happily, most small dogs have a better way to fly: specially designed carry-on luggage. Your dog can fly with you, safely and securely tucked underneath the seat. Follow these tips for safer and easier travel.

Carry-On Bags. Several companies make soft-sided, airline-approved

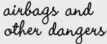

airbags and other dangers

When an airbag goes off, it can easily kill a small child. It can also kill a small dog. If you have front-seat airbags, be sure that your dog always travels in the back seat. Of course, by far the safest form of travel for your little dog is a comfortable crate. A loose pooch in the car is a possible hazard to driving and is in real danger if you're in a car accident.

carry-on bags for dogs and cats. These bags look very much like any carry-on luggage, except for the netting that gives your pet ventilation. Few other passengers will even notice that you're carrying a dog on board.

You can purchase these carriers at pet supply stores or on-line. Be sure that the particular bag you select is labeled as meeting airline size requirements.

Train Before You Travel. These bags are basically portable, lightweight dog crates. If you've crate trained your dog and if he rides in a crate in your car, he should quickly and easily adjust to his airline carrier.

As soon as you know you might be traveling, get your dog acclimated to his carry-on bag. Just as you did with his crate, help your dog view his bag as a happy haven.

Give him treats in the bag. Zip him in the bag and carry him around the house, giving him treats. Take him for some car rides in his bag, ending up at fun destinations, such as a park or his favorite pet store to buy a toy.

Book the Flight. Airlines charge for pets in the cabin, and most restrict the number of animals per flight to one or two. So, as soon as you know that you'll be traveling, call the airline and make arrangements for your pet to fly with you.

Unlike other carry-on luggage, it costs to tote your dog. Although it might be tempting to cheat and not tell anyone you have a dog on board, don't try it. You don't want to be stranded at the airport with airline agents telling you that your dog will have to fly cargo. With today's security measures, you're likely to have to show the ticketing information for the dog in order to get on the plane.

Check with the airline for any additional requirements. You may need to have a current health certificate for your dog, which you can get from your veterinarian.

What If...

Surprisingly, most dogs do incredibly well on planes. They curl up in the carrier and snooze through the trip.

There are a few precautions you'll want to plan for ahead of time that can prevent problems or can help you deal with the occasional dog that doesn't like traveling.

1. Unless you're traveling with a young puppy, have the dog skip breakfast and water the morning of the flight. You don't want a dog that really, really needs to potty at 30,000 feet. (If you are traveling with a puppy or other dog that

needs frequent meals, consult with your veterinarian.)

2. Potty your dog at the airport just before you check in. (Aren't you glad you taught him to potty on command?) If you're traveling with a puppy or dog that may need to pee during the trip, put a belly band on the dog.

3. If you are concerned that your dog might be likely to bark or whine because he is afraid, talk with your veterinarian about a mild sedative. While tranquilizing isn't advised for dogs who travel in cargo (they need to be alert enough to get on their feet if the baggage shifts around), you'll be there to keep an eye on your dog in the cabin. You can also consider getting a non-narcotic calming formula from a health store, such as Rescue Remedy™ or valerian root, but be careful with the dosage.

4. If you think your active dog will be bored, be sure to give him a lot of exercise before you take off. You'll be hanging out at the airport for a couple of hours, so use the time to take him on a walk from one corner of the airport to the next. You'll both feel better. Put a chew toy in his carrier so he'll have something to do during the flight.

Enjoy! Many small dog cross the country—and even the oceans—every day. Most of these frequent flyers take the travel happily in stride.

Japanese Chin

13 Easy Tricks and Games

Small dogs love to play games and to please you. They're perfect trick dogs because they look so adorable when they do these little stunts. Trick training is especially good for dogs who live in apartments and other small spaces, because these activities keep their minds busy and take no equipment and no space. Have a blast!

Wave, Shake, and Gimme Five

Wave is easy and fun to teach. It's also an especially good trick for shy dogs or to use in situations when you don't want a person grabbing at your small dog, since the person has to stand back to wave at your dog. Safety note: Wave and its variations are great tricks for dogs of any physical ability and any temperament.

Your dog will enjoy learning to wave.

1. TEACHING WAVE

Let your dog see you put a treat in your hand, then wrap the treat in a fist. Hold your fist near your dog's paws. Soon, your dog will start pawing at your fist, basically saying, "Give me that treat!"

As soon as his little paws start scratching at your hand, say, "Good wave!" and give him the treat. It takes most dogs just a few minutes to figure out this trick, since it rewards their natural impulse to "dig" for food.

Soon, you can put your fist near him, and say, "Wave!" and he'll paw at you. Now that he's figured out the basics, the next step is to tell him to sit, and hold your fist just a bit out of reach. He'll have to reach out with his paw. Look, he's waving! Over time, hold your hand farther and farther away. You can also gradually change the fist into a waving hand.

Pogo loves to wave, and it's handy with his animal-assisted therapy work. When it's time to leave a child's room, and if the child is a little hesitant for us to go, we have Pogo wave goodbye. It makes for a happy departure!

2. GIMME FIVE

Teach your dog to give a "high five" after he's learned to wave. When he waves, put your palm on his pads and say, "Gimme five!" Your dog will be a hip dude in a matter of minutes, since this is really just waving with a twist.

3. SHAKE

Okay, "high five" is a little California surf-style for some dogs. If your little dog is more the corporate executive type, teach him "Shake." When your dog is very sure of himself on the wave, reach out and gently take his paw, and say, "Good shake." Give him a big treat right away so that he thinks shaking is fun.

4. Say Please (Begging is Just Too Degrading)

Lots of small dogs naturally sit up to ask for things. For these dogs, "Say Please" is easy to teach. Safety note: This trick is not appropriate for any dog with back problems or for breeds that are prone to back problems. If you have a long-backed breed, such as a Dachshund or a Corgi, please don't teach this to your dog.

Ask your dog to sit. Hold the treat about an inch higher than you would for sit. When your dog reaches up, say, "Good Say Please!"

Some dogs learn "Say Please" in stages, and that's fine. At first your dog may just pick one paw off the ground—reward that. Later, he might pick up both just a little—reward whatever he does.

sit first

Make sure you teach "Say Please" after you have a solid sit command, or soon your sit will never include all four feet on the ground!

Most dogs will soon sit up if you hold the reward high enough and directly over their noses. In fact, the majority of dogs learn this trick in one or two sessions.

5. Walk Like a Man (and Dance, Dance, Dance)

Lots of small dogs naturally walk on their hind feet. (I actually know some small-breed male dogs who stand on their front paws and do a handstand while they pee against a tree so they seem taller, but we aren't going to teach that!) Walking on hind feet is really just an extension of "Say Please." This trick requires the dog to develop muscles he doesn't use in regular dog walking, so just ask for a couple of steps at first and gradually work your way up to longer walks or dances.

Safety note: Like "Say Please," this trick puts some strain on your dog's back. It is not appropriate for dogs with back problems or breeds prone to back problems, such as Dachshunds and Corgis.

Instead of holding the treat just an inch above your dog's nose, hold it a few inches above, so the dog has to stand on his hind feet to get the treat. Say, "Walk like a man!" or "Be a bear!" when your dog walks forward. Teach "Dance!" by asking your dog to walk in a circle on his back feet.

6. Sad Dog!

Don't worry, your dog won't be sad when he does this trick—he'll just look sad! Think of all those Hollywood dogs. When the director wants to show the dog's heart is breaking, what does he do? He has the dog lie down and put his sad little face on the floor. Safety note: This is a trick that's appropriate for any breed in any physical condition.

This is an easy trick to teach if your dog has a reliable down. Just hold the cookie to the floor, and when he puts his head down to get the cookie, say, "Sad dog" in a quiet, slow voice that stretches out the syllables (as in "saaaaaaaaad dooooooooooog"). If you keep your voice low and slow, he's likely to keep his head down. If you make your voice happy and high, he's likely to look up.

When teaching "walk" or "dance," start slowly and allow your dog to develop the muscles he'll need for these exercises.

If your dog doesn't understand what you're asking for, place him on a chair (one of the things that makes life easier with little dogs) and put the treat below the edge of the chair. Position him so that his chin rests on the edge of the chair when he's reaching down for the treat.

7. Play Dead (or Take a Nap)

This trick is taught the same way you teach Dachshunds the down command. With the dog standing, hold a treat next to his elbow. *Slowly* move the treat from the dog's elbow to his shoulder blade. Your dog will have to move his shoulders around to follow the treat and will lie down on his side. When he goes into the "dead" position, tell him he's a very, very good boy, say, "Good dead!" and give him the treat. Once he reliably follows your hand with the treat in it, ask him to play dead—if he rolls on his side, give him a big reward.

There are lots of variations on the Play Dead command. The most popular one is substituting the word "Bang!" for "Dead." After the dog has learned the action of rolling on his side, hold your finger like a toy gun, and say, "Bang"—the dog rolls over, dead. I have to admit I feel queasy just playing dead! Because I'm a non-violent, sensitive soul, I tell my dog, "Nap time!" It makes me feel better!

8. Roll Over

This trick is safe for dogs of almost any breed or physical condition, except dogs with back pain. However, while many dogs learn this trick easily and enjoy it,

This little dog is learning to roll over.

worried dogs may not enjoy the Roll Over. It puts them in the very vulnerable position of being on their backs, with their tummies exposed, in public. Yikes! That's sort of the doggie equivalent of performing naked. If your dog thinks this is fun, great. If he doesn't seem to want to play this game, that's okay, too. There are plenty of other tricks to learn.

Roll Over is just a continuation of Play Dead. The dog is lying on his side in the "dead" position. Just continue holding the cookie in front of his nose, and he'll make a complete turn on the floor.

9. Leap Into My Arms

This is a trick that your friends with Labradors and Golden Retrievers can't do. It's incredibly snazzy when your little dog seems to leap straight into your arms. This trick goes so quickly that you may not notice that the dog isn't really jumping into the person's arms; he's really jumping into the person's lap and is then scooped up into the person's arms. This trick is safe for dogs with the ability to easily and comfortably jump. Remember, your dog is only jumping as high as your lap, not clear up into your arms.

First, stand next to a wall, with your back firmly against the wall. Slide down until you're in a sitting position; your back is supported by the wall. Ask your dog to jump up on your lap, just like he does if you're sitting on the sofa.

When he is comfortable jumping on your lap, stand up slightly, making your lap smaller. Over time, continue to stand up straighter and straighter, until you're away from the wall, and just bent over a bit. As your lap gets smaller, be sure to scoop up your little dog comfortably and securely so he feels safe!

If you work into this trick gradually, you and your dog can have a lot of fun together. As your dog flies into your arms, this trick shows the spirit of how much you love each other.

10. Creating Your Own Tricks

Dogs offer behaviors all the time. Any activity that your dogs do consistently, you can label and turn into a trick. Just follow the principle of "catching your dog doing something right." When the dog does something fun, say, "Good!" or "Yes!" and reward it with a treat when possible. Soon, your dog will offer the behavior. Be careful what you ask your dog to do. It's one thing for a dog to joyfully do something on his own; it's another to do it because you ask. Dogs under about a year of age should never be required to jump on command. Any command that takes physical strain should first include a warm-up of running or playing to make sure that your pooch doesn't pull a muscle or otherwise injure himself. Keep your dog's safety the number-one priority!

My dogs taught themselves to do a food imitation: Popcorn! Most Papillons have the habit of leaping up and down, straight into the air. When they did this, I said, "Popcorn! Good!" and I'd laugh, clap, and give them a treat if I had it. Because they naturally liked the behavior, they quickly learned that "Popcorn" meant that they got to jump up and down—one of their natural

Be creative when teaching your dog tricks; here, three Papillons perform a popcorn imitation.

hobbies! When all three dogs do "Popcorn" at the same time, it really does look like a popper full of dancing little kernels.

Catch your dog doing something right, and you can have unique, enjoyable tricks!

Games in the House

Your little guy's brain works just as well (and maybe better!) than the big bruiser who lives next door. Let your dog enjoy some mental stimulation. Happily, your pocket-sized pooch can enjoy himself in your home, even if it's a small apartment. Here are a few games that you and your dog can do together without leaving the comfort of home.

11. FIND ME

You hide, and your dog seeks. If you have a friend or family member to hold the dog while you hide, that's great. If you've taught your dog a reliable stay, that will also give you time to hide, and you can play solo!

Start out by "hiding" where your dog can easily find you. Walk just around the corner. Maybe let him see your arm or toe. Then call him to you and reward him with play and hugs and maybe a treat. Over time, hide in more and more difficult areas, such as behind a door, in the closet, or in the upstairs bathtub.

This game hones your dog's skills and teaches him to keep track of you. And it's a ton of fun for you both.

12. WHICH HAND?

This trick teaches your dog to think with his nose. Even flat-faced Pugs or Pekingese have a much better sense of smell than us humans.

Take a favorite treat, and put it behind your back. Place it in one hand and then hold both fists in front of your dog. Ask him, "Which hand?" If he guesses right, he gets the treat. If he guesses wrong, show him what he missed, and say, "Try again!"

Most dogs quickly figure out to sniff and find the yummy treat in the correct hand. By the way, different dogs find this an amusing game for different lengths of time. A Beagle might find this fun all day long, while a dog with less of an orientation to his nose and less appetite might find just a few times enough.

Make sure that the game always ends with the dog finding the treat. He needs to know that he wins when he plays this game!

13. WHERE IS IT?

Take a favorite toy or a treat and let your dog see you put it under a washcloth. Ask him, "Where is it?" When he digs and gets it, let him have the treat or play with the toy. Begin to make the toy or treat just a little hard to find. Put it under your pillow or under the bed. Lead up to the point that you can put the toy or treat anywhere in the room when your dog isn't looking, and he'll find it.

These kinds of fun and games with your dog are only limited by your imagination. Your dog thrives on puzzles and play. He'll bond with you more closely when you do activities like this together, and you don't even have to leave your home to have a rousing good time with your little friend.

Cavalier King Charles Spaniel

Cool Stuff to Do With Your Trained Dog

The AKC Canine Good Citizen Test

*W*hoever thought up the American Kennel Club's Good Citizen test is a genius. (Well, knowing the AKC, it was probably a committee, so it was a committee of geniuses.) This test evaluates practical, useful skills, such as walking politely on a loose leash, accepting petting and grooming, and staying under control when there's another dog nearby. With some training, any dog has the ability to pass this practical test. Although it is administered through the AKC, dogs don't have to be purebred to earn the Canine Good Citizen (CGC) designation.

There can be practical reasons to earn a CGC. Some communities, apartments, and condominiums will allow only dogs with CGCs. It's also just plain fun. When you pass, you can send away for a nifty, official certificate that you can frame and hang in the hallway. And it's proper to put CGC after your dog's name. (We're all more impressive with initials after our names!)

Most importantly, it's proof to yourself and others that you and your dog accomplished something together. You have a trained and reliable dog who is an asset to your community. That's something in which you should take pride.

Check with local dog trainers or humane organizations to find Canine Good Citizen testing in your community. Some events are also listed at the AKC website found in the Resources section of this book. The training outlined in this book was designed with the AKC CGC test in mind. Here are the requirements for the CGC test and some hints on preparing for it. I hope you'll go out and take the test. Your dog can do this! (Note: The material below is from the AKC; the comments in italics are the author's.)

AKC CANINE GOOD CITIZEN TEST REQUIREMENTS
Test Item 1: Accepting a friendly stranger: This test demonstrates that the dog will allow a friendly stranger to approach it and speak to the handler in a natural,

everyday situation. The evaluator walks up to the dog and handler and greets the handler in a friendly manner, ignoring the dog. The evaluator and handler shake hands and exchange pleasantries. The dog must show no sign of resentment or shyness, and must not break position or try to go to the evaluator.

This one is pretty easy! If your dog is worried around strangers, give him a job to do by asking him to sit and stay.

Test Item 2: Sitting politely for petting: This test demonstrates that the dog will allow a friendly stranger to touch it while it is out with its handler. To begin the exercise, the evaluator pets the dog on the head and body, with the dog sitting at the handler's side. The handler may talk to his or her dog throughout the exercise. The dog may stand in place as it is petted. The dog must not show shyness or resentment.

The most important thing to keep in mind is to communicate with your dog when you're taking this test. It's fine to remind him to sit and stay—and to tell him he's a good boy.

Test Item 3: Appearance and grooming: This practical test demonstrates that the dog will welcome being groomed and examined and will permit someone, such as a veterinarian, groomer, or friend of the owner, to do so. It also demonstrates the owner's care, concern and sense of responsibility. The evaluator inspects the dog to determine if it is clean and groomed. The dog must appear to be in healthy condition (i.e., proper weight, clean, healthy and alert). The handler should supply the comb or brush commonly used on the dog. The evaluator then softly combs or brushes the dog, and in a natural manner, lightly examines the ears and gently picks up each front foot. It is not necessary for the dog to hold a specific position during the examination, and the handler may talk to the dog, praise it and give encouragement throughout.

You'll be glad that you did all the touching exercises with your dog. Assuming your dog knows the names of his body parts, reassure your dog by telling him, "They're going to look at your ears. Good ears! And your feet—good feet!"

Test Item 4: Out for a walk (walking on a loose lead): This test demonstrates that the handler is in control of the dog. The dog may be on either side of the handler. The dog's position should leave no doubt that the dog is attentive to the handler and is responding to the handler's movements and changes of direction. The dog need not be perfectly aligned with the handler and need not sit when the handler stops.

The evaluator may use a pre-plotted course or may direct the handler/dog team by issuing instructions or commands. In either case, there should be a right turn, left turn, and an about turn with at least one stop in between and another at the end. The handler may talk to the dog along the way, praise the dog, or give commands in a normal tone of voice. The handler may sit the dog at the halts if desired.

Remember to praise and encourage your dog during the test. That's what's most likely to keep him calm and near you.

Test Item 5: Walking through a crowd: This test demonstrates that the dog can move about politely in pedestrian traffic and is under control in public places. The dog and handler walk around and pass close to several people (at least three). The dog may show some interest in the strangers but should continue to walk with the handler, without evidence of overexuberance, shyness, or resentment. The handler may talk to the dog and encourage or praise the dog throughout the test. The dog should not jump on people in the crowd or strain on the leash.

Activities, like the American Kennel Club's Canine Good Citizen test, give you and your pet the opportunity to reach a goal together.

Again, talk with your dog. It will keep him focused on you and help him have a good time while he aces this test.

Test Item 6: Sit and down on command and staying in place: This test demonstrates that the dog has training, will respond to the handler's commands to sit and down, and will remain in the place commanded by the handler (sit or down position, whichever the handler prefers). Prior to this test, the dog's leash is replaced with a 20-foot long line. The handler may take a reasonable amount of time and use more than one command to get the dog to sit and then down. The evaluator must determine if the dog has responded to the handler's commands. The handler may not force the dog into position but may touch the dog to offer gentle guidance.

When instructed by the evaluator, the handler tells the dog to stay and walks forward the length of the line, turns and returns to the dog at a natural pace. The dog must remain in the place in which it was left (it may change position) until the evaluator instructs the handler to release the dog. The dog may be released from the front or the side.

This is the exercise that's most commonly failed. Practice your sits, downs, and stays before you take the test.

Test Item 7: Coming when called: This test demonstrates that the dog will come when called by the handler. The handler will walk 10 feet from the dog, turn to face the dog, and call him. The handler may use encouragement to get the dog to come. Handlers may choose to tell dogs to "stay" or "wait," or they may simply walk away, giving no instructions to the dog.

Remember the advice that you learned in the very beginning: Be more interesting than a squirrel, and praise, praise, praise your dog for coming to you.

Test Item 8: Reaction to another dog: This test demonstrates that the dog can behave politely around other dogs. Two handlers and their dogs approach each other from a distance of 20 to 30 feet, stop, shake hands and exchange pleasantries, and continue on for about 10 feet. The dogs should show no more than casual interest in each other. Neither dog should go to the other dog or its handler.

The best way to keep your dog from approaching another is to give him a specific command. When you stop, ask your dog to "sit" and "stay," then shake hands. The evaluator will have a "neutral" dog available for this test that is safe, trained, and reliable.

Test Item 9: Reaction to distraction: This test demonstrates that the dog is confident at all times when faced with common distracting situations. The evaluator will select and present two distractions. Examples of distractions include dropping a chair, rolling a crate dolly past the dog, having a jogger run in front of the dog, or dropping a crutch or cane.

The dog may express natural interest and curiosity and/or may appear slightly startled but should not panic, try to run away, show aggressiveness, or bark. The handler may talk to the dog and encourage or praise it throughout the exercise.

This is a good time to use the "watch me!" command.

Test Item 10: Supervised separation: This test demonstrates that a dog can be left with a trusted person, if necessary, and will maintain training and good manners. Evaluators are encouraged to say something like, "Would you like me to watch your dog?" and then take hold of the dog's leash. The owner will go out of sight for three minutes. The dog does not have to stay in position but should not continually bark, whine, or pace unnecessarily, or show anything stronger than mild agitation or nervousness.

I like this part of the test, even though some dogs find it difficult. Think of being out with friends and saying, "I have to use the bathroom, would you watch my dog?" You want your dog to be comfortable in that circumstance, and this test makes sure you prepare your dog for such everyday life occurrences.

Equipment: All tests must be performed on leash. Dogs should wear well-fitting buckle or slip collars made of leather, fabric, or chain. Special training collars such as pinch collars, head halters, etc. are not permitted in the CGC test. The AKC recognizes that special training collars may be very useful tools for beginning dog trainers; however, they feel that dogs are ready to take the CGC test at the point at which they are transitioned to regular collars. The evaluator supplies a 20-foot lead for the test. The owner/handler should bring written proof of rabies vaccines and the dog's brush or comb to the test.

Encouragement: Owners/handlers may use praise and encouragement throughout the test. The owner may pet the dog between exercises. Food and treats are not permitted during testing, nor is the use of toys, squeaky toys, etc. to get the dog to do something. We recognize that food and toys may provide valuable reinforcement or encouragement during the training process, but these items should not be used during the test.

Failures/Dismissals: Any dog that eliminates during testing must be marked failed. The only exception to this rule is that elimination is allowable in test Item 10, but only when test Item 10 is held outdoors. Any dog that growls, snaps, bites, attacks, or attempts to attack a person or another dog is not a good citizen and must be dismissed from the test.

Becoming a Therapy Dog

My dog, Pogo, is a Delta Society Pet Partner therapy dog. I've done a wide array of great activities with my dogs over the years, including competitive obedience and dabbling in events such as herding, earthdog, and flyball. Of all the rewarding, even exhilarating things I've done with my animals, for me nothing comes close to therapy work.

There is a significant need for small therapy dogs. While every dog (and cat, bird, and other creature) who performs this work brings something special to the task, our small dogs' abilities to sit on beds and laps have a charm that a big dog can't match. Also, some people who are afraid of large dogs enjoy the company of a small one.

There is an endless variety of settings in which to perform this important work: hospitals, hospices, nursing homes, schools, libraries. You and your dog will find a

Your well-trained companion will enjoy hugs from you and might even be a good therapy dog candidate.

niche that you both enjoy. Pogo decided that he wanted to work with children. Frankly, I was always sort of scared of kids, but Pogo made it clear that's what he was made to do. Now, we visit regularly at Legacy Emanuel Children's Hospital in Portland, and I wouldn't trade the experiences for the world.

Therapy work isn't for every dog. Just as every person isn't cut out to be a social worker, every dog isn't cut out to be a therapy dog. People who evaluate therapy dogs estimate that about 25 to 30 percent of trained dogs enjoy this work. (My other two dogs are just as well-trained as Pogo, but they'd rather sleep with a cobra than be hugged by a small child!) The three major therapy organizations, which are listed in the Resources section of this book, have certified over 20,000 animals to do this work. Each organization has differing requirements, so check with them about their procedures. If your dog might enjoy this work, I hope you'll try it. You might find it changes your life!

THE DELTA SOCIETY APTITUDE TEST

Most therapy organizations give a modified, tougher version of the AKC Canine Good Citizen test. They include medical equipment and distractions as part of the test. Delta Society does that as well, but also has a second part of the test, in which the dog's temperament is given a tough test. I like these extra requirements. In my own experiences, every one of these extra tests, especially hugging and weird petting, happens in real therapy visits on a daily basis. I'm glad that my dog and I were prepared. Even if you choose to be certified with another organization, I highly recommend you train your dog to be comfortable with the Delta Society Aptitude Test. (Note: The material below is from the Delta Society; the comments in italics are the author's.)

Exercise A: Overall Exam: This exercise demonstrates that the animal will accept and is comfortable being examined by a stranger, and that the handler knows how to present the animal on a visit and how to help the animal accept and welcome being touched all over.

The evaluator will pet your dog nicely, but thoroughly. Aren't you glad your dog enjoys all that touching by now?

Exercise B: Exuberant and Clumsy Petting: This exercise demonstrates that the animal will maintain self-control and will tolerate clumsy petting by people who have differing physical abilities or who do not know proper etiquette around the animal, and that the handler can work with the animal to help it tolerate such attention.

The evaluator will probably pet your dog with his or her knuckles and elbows. The evaluator won't hurt your dog but will look for signs of stress. One visit with a kid whose hands are in casts or an elderly person with hands frozen in place, and you'll see the value of this exercise.

Exercise C: Restraining Hug: This exercise demonstrates that the animal will accept or welcome restraint, and that the handler can assist the animal to accept or welcome such a situation.

This can be a tough exercise for a little dog! It's also a realistic one, especially for a little dog doing therapy work. Practice by letting people hold your dog from the day he comes into your home. Make sure he learns to enjoy happy, appropriate interactions with people who are holding him. Before the test, make sure you practice having friends hug him, and then laugh and give the dog a treat. Make hugging strangers a funny game for your small dog.

Exercise D: Staggering, Gesturing Individual: This exercise demonstrates that the animal will exhibit confidence when a person acting in an unusual manner approaches and then interacts with it, and the handler has the social skills to interact with such a person while attending to the animal.

The Delta Society allows very small dogs (about 10 pounds and under) to do some exercises in the handler's arms. Decide ahead of time which exercises you want to do on the floor and which are best in your arms. (Talk with the evaluator to discuss this at the beginning of your evaluation.) When Pogo and I took the test, I decided that, in real life, I would hold him in situations like Exercises D, E, F, and G. That was fine with the evaluator. In our therapy work, I definitely hold him when the environment around us seems at all chaotic.

The Delta Society test evaluates both the handler and the dog, so remember to interact with the people who are role-playing in these exercises.

Exercise E: Angry Yelling: This exercise demonstrates that the animal will not be upset when someone exhibits angry emotions, and that the handler can help the animal tolerate such a situation.

The yelling will take place several feet from your dog. Remember, you're allowed to talk with your dog during the test. Tell him quietly that he's fine. When the yelling is over, your dog is expected to accept petting from these people. Smile and relax. Your body language and words will tell your dog he's just fine.

Exercise F: Bumped from Behind: This exercise demonstrates that the animal is able to recover when a person bumps into it, and that the handler can not only tolerate the animal being bumped, but can also assist the animal to recover.

For small dogs, being bumped while they're standing on the floor can be pretty scary. It's a lot different for a Chihuahua to have a bump than a Golden Retriever! I like to take this part of the test with my small dog in my arms.

Exercise G: Crowded and Petted by Several People: This exercise demonstrates that the animal will tolerate crowding and petting by several people at once, and that the handler has the social skills to visit with a group of people while still attending to the animal and maintaining its well-being.

This experience happens very frequently to therapy dogs! When I've seen the test given, there's been a person in a wheelchair, one standing, and one kneeling, and all grabbing (gently) at the dog.

Exercise H: Leave It: This exercise demonstrates the animal will ignore a toy left on the floor.

"Leave it" is a very important command in therapy situations. Imagine if your dog sees a pill he wants to swallow!

Exercise I: Offered a Treat: This exercise demonstrates the animal will take a treat politely and gently.

After all he's been through, this shows just what a good sport your dog is!

Exercise J: Overall Assessment: This item determines that the handler is proactive, not reactive or inactive, in the handling and management of his/her animal.

The evaluator will talk with you about your dog's (and your) strengths and weaknesses as individuals and as a team.

my therapy experiences

I have never been more touched in my life than when seeing Pogo relate to sick children. Here's one personal story that happened recently. (The child's name has been changed to protect confidentiality, but the experience is 100-percent real.)

Pogo and I could hear the wheezing of the toddler's breath before we could see Ashley's tiny body in the crib. Her mom told us that she'd had extensive throat surgery the day before, and every breath was hurting her. Pogo's body tensed with each painful breath. His eyes looked back and forth from the little girl to me.

"Is he afraid?" asked Ashley's mother.

I looked carefully at Pogo's face. There was no fear—just concern. "He's fine," I said. "He's just worried for her."

So we put Pogo in Ashley's crib. He quickly settled in, snuggling against her leg. Almost instantly, we could see her calm down. Her hands relaxed. She looked up at her mother and smiled. Suddenly, Ashley's breathing got much more ragged. She started to cough. Pogo sat up abruptly, worried again.

"Don't worry," the mom told Pogo. "The doctors have wanted her to cough. We've been here two days and she hasn't coughed like she was supposed to. Not until now." As quickly as the coughing began, it ended.

Pogo lay down and settled next to Ashley again. He relaxed against her legs and reached out and put his paw on her arm. His eyes were at half-mast, with that dreamy look he gets when he seems to be consciously healing a child. Ashley's eyes closed and she fell asleep.

Her mom's eyes were on the monitor. "Look," she whispered, pointing to the monitor. I saw rhythmic waves of heart and breath measurements etched in yellow on the black screen.

"Ashley's breathing is better than it's been since the surgery. She's breathing better with Pogo than she had been on the oxygen." The mom and I stared at the monitor for a few minutes, taking it in.

Pogo didn't need a high-tech machine to tell him how Ashley was doing. His heartbeat measured her heartbeat; his slow breath was in rhythm with hers. She moved in her sleep, snuggling closer to my dog, relaxed and content.

Competitive Obedience

If you think obedience is boring, go watch an obedience trial. You just might change your mind. This sport, especially with today's positive training methods, is full of tail-wagging fun. It's a happy, bonding experience to show off all the work you've done together and to get some titles. (Some of the things you'll need to learn are covered in Chapter 11: Advanced Obedience Training.)

The AKC limits competition to purebred dogs. If you have a purebred, unregistered dog, you may still be able to compete at AKC trials, through their Indefinite Listing Privilege, which allows spayed and neutered dogs who are clearly purebred to compete in performance events. Don't fret if you have a mixed breed! The UKC (United Kennel Club) welcomes spayed or neutered mixed breeds. The UKC is a respected and reputable organization that has titles that are equivalent to the AKC. Obedience dogs work at the following three levels:

NOVICE OBEDIENCE

At the Novice level, dogs earn a Companion Dog (CD) title. You'll have a qualified judge giving you commands. Dogs must heel on- and off-leash in a pattern that includes left turns, right turns, fast pace, slow pace, and halts. You'll heel in a figure-eight pattern around two people. The dog must stand for examination while the judge touches him lightly on the head, shoulders, and back. He must stay while you leave him, then call him, and he must come running and sit in front of you. He then finishes back into the heel position on your left side.

After the individual exercises are complete, all the dogs from the class come back together into the ring for the long sit (one minute) and long down (three minutes) while the handlers stand at the other end of the ring. Your dog must pass these requirements at three different shows (earning a "leg" at each show) to earn his Companion Dog (CD) title.

OPEN OBEDIENCE

At the Open level, dogs earn a Companion Dog Excellent (CDX) title. All Open work is done off-leash. The dog heels and does a figure-eight, as in the Novice Class. On the recall exercise, you leave the dog, call him, and (on the judge's signal) tell him to "down" as he's running to you. Then you complete the come exercise as in Novice. He retrieves a dumbbell across the ring and over a high jump. ("High" is a relative term, because it's the height of your dog at the shoulder. Your "high" jump might be 8 inches tall, but that's high for a Pomeranian!) He also jumps over some low, flat boards. In the long-stay exercises, all the dogs in the class come back together into the ring for the long sit (three minutes) and long down (five minutes) while the handlers leave the building (or are taken out of sight). After passing three times, your dog earns the Companion Dog Excellent (CDX) title.

UTILITY

Utility is the most advanced work. All commands are off-leash. The dog heels as in Novice, but must work entirely on hand signals. You'll follow the heeling with a series of signals that require the dog to stand, stay, down, come, and finish. You'll have leather and metal dumbbells; your dog must select the items you touch from those you don't. The judge will put out three gloves; your dog must retrieve the glove that you point to. In the moving stand exercise, you'll heel, then tell your dog "stay" as you continue forward; the judge will touch your dog all over, and then you'll call your dog back to the heel position. The final exercise is the most dramatic: You'll send your dog away from you across the ring where there will be a solid high jump on one side and a bar jump on the other. You'll tell the dog to jump over whichever jump the judge designates. Then you'll send him back to jump the other one. After passing three times, your dog will earn the respected and coveted Utility Dog (UD) title.

Advanced obedience classes include jumping, retrieving, hand signals, and finding things by scent.

Small dogs of every breed have earned this title—so can yours!

UDX AND OTCH

Utility dogs that go on competing and pass both Open and Utility at 10 shows after they earn their UD title earn the Utility Dog Excellent (UDX) title. In these classes that are limited to dogs with advanced titles, dogs earn points on a designated scale for defeating other dogs. After a dog earns 100 points, he earns the highest title in obedience: Obedience Trial Champion (OTCh).

(Note: The exercises described reflect the AKC regulations. UKC requirements are similar and equivalent, but vary slightly from the AKC rules.)

Competitive obedience is an enjoyable hobby for both you and your dog. It's lots of fun showing off the intelligence and versatility of our little dogs! To learn more about training your small dog for obedience competition, read *Competitive Obedience Training for the Small Dog* by Barbara Cecil and Gerianne Darnell. They've also put this information into an excellent set of videos. To find a competition trainer, go to a local dog show; most conformation shows also have an obedience trial. Watch the people and dogs who are smiling and having a good time, and find out where they train.

Other Fun Sports

Once you have a foundation of basic obedience, there is a world of activities waiting for you and your dog. Try them! You'll find fun, adventures, and friends. Plus, there's nothing more adorable than a small dog doing a big job! Here are a few sports to consider with your convenient-sized competitor.

AGILITY

Today, agility is America's most popular dog sport. It's no wonder: This is about as much fun as a dog can have with his fur on. Dogs run through an

obstacle course, flying over hurdles (set as low as 8 inches for small dogs), climbing up A-frames, skipping along dog walks (elevated balance beams), and careening through above-ground tunnels.

While dogs must be purebred to compete in AKC competitions, other sponsoring organizations welcome mixed breeds, with certain requirements. Learn more about this great sport by checking out the sponsoring organizations, all found in the Resources section.

After your dog has mastered basic obedience training, try a more challenging dog sport, like agility.

RALLY OBEDIENCE

Rally Obedience is something of a hybrid between traditional competitive obedience and agility. The dog heels through a course full of weave poles, tricky turns, and occasional low jumps. It's a fun, interactive sport that's just starting as a competitive event.

FLYBALL

Flyball is a relay race, with four dogs flying over hurdles, hitting a box that dispenses tennis balls (tiny tennis balls for tiny dogs!), and carrying the tennis balls back to the handler. This sport is on fast-forward! Flyball teams are all looking for small dogs (called "height dogs"), since they jump lower hurdles if they have a small dog on their team.

EARTHDOG

If you have a terrier or a Dachshund, earthdog may be the sport for you. Your dog will go through underground tunnels in search of rats. (Don't worry—the rats are safely in cages. The dogs can't hurt the rats, and the rats can't hurt the dogs.)

HERDING

Okay, strictly speaking, herding isn't a small dog's sport. There aren't any official organizations that give little dogs herding titles. (Corgis can earn herding titles, but they're medium-sized dogs on short legs.) However, lots of small dogs love to herd. Don't endanger them by herding sheep—let them herd ducks! Talk with people with herding breeds or go to a pet fair, and you might find the chance to let your dog show his serious instincts. It's a ton of fun!

My dog, Radar, thinks herding is what he was born to do. Sometimes, just to make him happy, I take him to a place where dogs are trained to herd and let him move the ducks from place to place. He loves it!

DANCING WITH DOGS

The dog sport that's got everyone talking is Canine Freestyle, or dancing with dogs. You pick the music and the costumes, and you and your dog dance together. Canine Freestyle allows you to select music and tricks that reflect your interests and your dog's size and abilities, which makes it a ton of fun. For more information, contact the World Canine Freestyle Organization.

Miniature Pinscher

Advanced Obedience Training

*I*f you've followed the lessons in the last section, you have a dog who's under control. He comes when called, walks pleasantly on a loose leash, and stays in place. That's terrific!

Sometimes it's fun to add a little flash to the basics. This section will do that, starting with the heel command. The heel exercise is when the dog walks perfectly next to the handler's left side, sitting squarely next to the handler whenever the handler stops. Done well, heeling is more like dancing together than merely walking; it's an orchestrated, coordinated movement of dog and handler.

Teaching a Small Dog to Heel

Part of the reason to teach a small dog a true obedience heel is just because it looks so cool, and using positive techniques, the dog thinks the exercise is a ton of fun. But there are some practical reasons to learn the exercise.

Imagine yourself with an armload of groceries on a hot day. You can't carry the dog and all the groceries. Wouldn't it be great to have a dog who walks perfectly at your left side, just inches from your feet, never leaving that position? Or imagine yourself walking downtown with your dog, and again your arms are full. Think how handy it would be to have a dog who would walk smartly by your side through the throngs of people, sitting every time you stop. If you think about it, there are a lot of times you can benefit from having that level of control over your dog.

In addition, heeling is a very major element in competitive obedience, which can be a great hobby for humans and their dogs. And it's just plain fun to teach your dog something very precise. It might as well be some snazzy heeling!

Teaching a small dog to heel is entirely different from teaching a full-sized dog the same exercise. If you've trained a larger dog with today's modern, positive training methods, you probably taught him to look at your face. If your 6-inch-tall

Yorkie tried to look up into your face, he'd develop neck strain! Instead, we teach small dogs to concentrate on a spot on your shin, just about even with his nose.

First, determine a target point on your shin that is level with your dog's nose. Don't have him looking up (bad for his back) or down. (Note: If your dog is still growing, you can't determine what his target point will be.) Don't teach a formal heel until he's reached his full height, usually by the time he's eight months old in small breeds. While you're waiting for him to be old enough to learn a formal heel, work on walking nicely on a loose leash, staying, coming, and other foundation blocks of obedience.

- Hold a treat at the target point. When your dog focuses on it, say, "Good heel!" and give him the treat.

- Once he's focusing on the target spot when you say, "Heel!" give him the command and take a small step. Reward him with the treat as he moves with you. (Use easily chewed treats so he doesn't stop and chew.) Start with a single step, then two—build up distance very gradually over time.

The competition sit means that your dog will sit perfectly by your side when you come to a halt, without the rocking motion associated with the traditional sit.

The Competition Sit

When you heel with your dog, you want him to sit perfectly at your side every time you come to a halt. This means teaching your dog to sit differently from the very beginning. You'll notice that in the traditional way of teaching a sit, your dog shifts his weight to his rear end and rocks backwards. If he was in the perfect heel position at your side when you stopped, this rocking motion would put him out of position, looking slightly less snazzy and losing you some points in obedience competition.

So, if you're even fantasizing about competing with your dog in obedience trials, you want to teach him the obedience sit instead of the rocking sit.

TEACHING THE COMPETITION SIT

- Hold the treat just in front of the dog's nose, just taller than the dog.

- When the dog reaches up to get the treat, gently tuck your finger just above the dog's hock (back knee) to go into a sit position. You'll see that he tucks his rear forward, rather than moving his front legs back, coming to a perfect competition sit.

Once your dog understands the heel exercise and separately sits by tucking up his butt underneath him, then you can combine the two. You're looking flashy now: You are walking proudly, with your dog in perfect sync with every step, and sitting pertly when you stop. It doesn't get any cuter than that for small dog lovers!

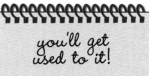

you'll get used to it!

If you've taught other dogs the rocking sit, the competition sit might feel a little awkward at first, but be persistent. Soon, this will become the regular way you teach your dogs to sit, and rocking them back will seem strange.

Stand for Examination

Just as the heel command is an orchestrated version of walking on a loose leash, the stand for examination exercise takes the concept of standing quietly for petting or a vet check and makes it a little more demanding.

In the stand for examination exercise, the handler tells the dog to stand, then leaves the dog in a stay while a judge touches the dog on the head, shoulders, and back. This exercise will build your dog's confidence, as long as you teach it gently and don't push your dog too hard, too fast.

TEACHING STAND FOR EXAMINATION

- With your dog sitting at your left side, step forward with your left leg and hold a treat at his nose level. When he takes the treat, say, "Good stand!" Practice just this part until your dog has figured out that when you say, "Stand," you want him to put himself on all four paws.

Build your dog's confidence with competitive exercises, such as the "stand for examination."

- When he is confident in the stand command, add "stay," and step in front of the dog. Give your dog a treat, saying, "Good stand! Good stay!"

- When your dog does a very reliable, relaxed stand-stay, have a friend (playing "judge") walk near the dog. Don't let the judge touch the dog until your little dog is very relaxed and comfortable with footsteps nearby. Remember, the stand for examination is much more demanding for a dog who's 10 inches tall than it is for one who's 25 inches tall—that human judge looms very high when you're vertically challenged!

Once your dog is secure in his stand-stay, have your judge friend gently touch the dog. The judge should go in and out quickly, not making eye contact and not holding her hand for the dog to sniff. It's easiest for the dog to stand still this way.

DEALING WITH CONFUSION

Frequently, dogs get confused. Does his handler want him to sit? To stand? To down? Much of this confusion comes when the handler holds the treat in the wrong place. In the beginning, where you hold the lure determines where your dog places his body. If your dog is sitting when he's supposed to stand, for example, you're probably holding the lure too high.

Front and Finish

You have already learned the basics of the come command. This exercise will give you more control of the end of that command. Officially, the come command is called the "recall." (I have trouble with this name, because it reminds me of a lemon car getting a recall notice. It's bad when cars are recalled, but it's *good* when dogs are!)

When you first teach your dog to come to you, you're just relieved that the little guy is headed toward you. After a while, though, you'd like the dog to be under the best possible control. The front command asks the dog to sit quietly at your toes at the end of the come command, and the finish command teaches him to move back to your left side.

TEACHING FRONT

The front command requires the dog to sit squarely in front of the handler. Happily, this is one of the easiest things to teach a dog. It's so easy that I usually include it in the very beginner's come command training.

- First, call the dog to you.

- When he's about halfway to you, bend over, keeping your knees straight, holding a treat in front of your legs. (Yes—more bending for small dog trainers!) Hold the treat just above your dog's nose level, at the same height you held it when teaching him to sit. Tell the dog to "sit" as he comes to you. When he sits squarely in front of you, give him the treat.

- Over time, straighten up and use the treat as a reward for him sitting at your feet at the end of the recall command.

TEACHING FINISH

If you watch gymnastics, you know that every routine has to have a dismount—a move that ends the routine. In dog obedience, that's the finish.

When the dog is in the front position, he's sitting smack dab in front of you. You want him to go back to your left side. The finish command returns your dog back to your left side. There are two finishes: the *swing* (where the dog makes a small circle to your left and sits) and the *around* (in which the dog walks to your right, goes around your back, and then sits on your left side).

To teach the *swing*: With the dog in the front position, hold the treat in your left hand. Take a step back with your left foot to encourage the dog to move, and lure the dog with the treat to your left side. He will do an about turn on your left side and come back into the heel position. Reward him when he comes to the heel position. Be sure the dog turns toward you in the swing; when you lure the dog, you're moving your arm in a counter-clockwise circle.

As your dog begins to understand the swing command, stop moving your left leg—stand still and let your dog do the moving.

"Around" has the same function as "swing:" to get the dog from your front to your left side. In the swing, the dog flips to your left side. In the around, the dog walks in a tight circle behind you from right to left.

To teach the *around*: With the dog in the front position, hold your treat in your right hand. Take a step back with your right leg to get the dog moving. Hold the treat in front of the dog and lure him around the back of your legs to your left side. Give him the treat when he's sitting at your left side. When your dog begins to understand the exercise, stop moving your right leg.

limber up!

Training a small dog will help make you more limber! It can be a challenge for those of us who aren't so slim and/or aren't so young to pass a doggie treat around our knees so our dogs can follow the lure. Just do the best you can—our dogs are very good at figuring out what we *meant* to do.

Communicating With Hand Signals

Every class I teach, someone asks, "When are we going to learn hand signals?" Hand signals are easy to teach your dog and help to keep the dog focused on you. It's nice if an older dog knows hand signals, because if his hearing begins to fade, you still have a great way to communicate. Plus, they look really cool—an important factor to consider!

Dogs naturally read body language, because they use their bodies to communicate a lot more than people do. Most dogs will notice your hand movements and respond quickly.

You can invent a hand signal for any exercise. It's easiest for the dog to learn a signal if it's an extension of the way you held the treat to lure the dog into the exercise in the first place. So, a sit signal becomes holding the palm of your hand above his head, which is an exaggerated form of the way you held the treat when you taught him to sit. Similarly, "stand" becomes a flat hand in front of his nose.

You can pair any signal with any command that your dog already knows. For example, if your little guy has a reliable down, and you want the signal for down to be a raised arm, just say, "Down" and raise your arm. He'll do his down command, but he'll notice that you're moving your arm. After you pair the voice command and the signal several times in a row, try using just the signal (raising your arm without the verbal command). Chances are he'll react to the hand signal and do the down. If he does, tell him, "Good down" and give him a big reward.

seeing is listening

The more easily your dog can see a hand signal, the better he can respond. Remember, he's down at your ankle level, so he might not notice gestures that you're making up by your shoulders. Think about his line of sight as you decide what signal you want to use for each exercise.

If he doesn't go down when you signal at first, it just means that he hasn't associated your raised arm with the down command yet. Continue to combine the hand signal with the verbal command, but occasionally try just the hand signal alone, until the dog figures it out.

Hand signals are a lot of fun, especially with small dogs. They look for all the world like little remote stuffed toys, merrily doing things across the room. If you train hand signals in a happy, positive way, they're a joy for your dog. You're really concentrating on each other, and that's what communication and rapport with your dog is all about.

Shih Tzu

Reflections on Life With Small Dogs

There isn't much in life that can be more joyful than spending time with your small dog. Because they are so portable, these dogs become even more a part of our lives than their larger cousins. We have the opportunity to learn from them and give to them in ways that no other dog can quite match. Here are a few thoughts I wanted to share about that awesome, powerful relationship.

- Every dog trainer can tell in class who has just had an argument with a spouse or who is worried about finances from the way they treat their dogs. Please think about your actions and choose not to take out your feelings on your little dog, even in subtle ways. Of course you aren't the kind of person who would hit or yell at your dog, but you might find yourself being short or a bit gruff with him when you're in a bad mood. You've asked your dog to share your intimate feelings—your very soul. It is exceptionally cruel to then turn and be angry or unpleasant to this little creature just because you're in a bad mood. If you're feeling blue, stop, take a breath, and connect with the happy little spirit on your lap. It will be good for both of you!

- Let your little dog be a dog. You don't need to go out to the country to do this—you can do it in your living room. Let him play, wrestle, and "kill" a toy. Let him sniff you out when you play hide-and-seek games. He is full of instinct and intelligence—give him the chance to use it. He'll live longer and be happier when he's allowed to play and think like a mini-wolf.

- Before you laugh at your dog's antics, think about whether they are funny. If your dog is growling and baring his teeth, he's feeling threatened. If he's shaking, he's probably afraid. Give him the leadership and gentle structure that he needs to feel confident. And when he's being silly and playing games with you, laugh with him. He'll appreciate your humor!

- Only use gentle training methods with your little dog. Come on; if the worst came to the worst, you can just pick him up! You don't need to use a choke collar or zap him with electricity. Have fun and feel good about who you are when you work with your dog.

- Be proud of your dog! Especially if you're a man, you may have had prejudice against little dogs all your life and find yourself surprised, and even embarrassed, to love one. Get over it! Your dog deserves to know that you are proud to be seen with him and that you think he's terrific. Walk with a smile on your face, and your dog will prance at your side. Who cares what other people think? You have a real dog—and the best dog in the world for *you*! What more could you ask of your dog?

- Be open to the wisdom that your dog has to teach you. When your little dog has the courage to bark at an intruder, appreciate what that loyalty means. If

The priceless bond you share with your small dog will last a lifetime.

your dog is gentle with a sick child, even though that child is three times as big as he is, think about the grace your dog is showing. When your small, shy dog trusts you enough to try new experiences, admire that courage. Think about how you can share your dog's admirable qualities. There is a saying that's attributed to British military dog trainers: "Let me be the person that my dog thinks I am."

- Remember that the best things really can come in small packages. You'll learn the very best small packages don't hold diamonds or the keys to a sports car. The best small packages are wrapped in fur and contain a heart that's as big as an ocean.

The small dog who is waiting for you at the door when you come home, who curls on your lap when you need solace, who looks you in the eye with love and wags his tail when you need company—that is the best small package you'll ever get. There isn't a better symbol of love, and that love will be renewed every day the two of you share.

Resources

ORGANIZATIONS

American Kennel Club (AKC)
5580 Centerview Drive
Raleigh, NC 27606
Telephone: (919) 233-9767
Fax: (919) 233-3627
E-mail: info@akc.org
www.akc.org

Association of Pet Dog Trainers (APDT)
5096 Sand Road SE
Iowa City, IA 52240-8217
Telephone: (800) PET-DOGS
Fax: (856) 439-0525
E-mail: information@apdt.com
www.apdt.com

Canadian Kennel Club (CKC)
89 Skyway Avenue, Suite 100
Etobicoke, Ontario
M9W 6R4
Telephone: (416) 675-5511
Fax: (416) 675-6506
E-mail: information@ckc.ca
www.ckc.ca

Delta Society
875 124th Ave. NE, Ste 101
Bellevue, WA 98005
Telephone: (425) 226-7357
Fax: (425) 235-1076
E-mail: info@deltasociety.org
www.deltasociety.org

International Agility Link (IAL)
Global Administrator: Steve
Drinkwater
E-mail: yunde@powerup.au
www.dogpatch.org/agility/IAL/ial.html

The Kennel Club
1 Clarges Street
London
W1J 8AB
Telephone: 0870 606 6750
Fax: 0207 518 1058
www.the-kennel-club.org.uk

North American Flyball Association (NAFA)
1400 West Devon Avenue #512
Chicago, IL 60660
Telephone: (800) 318-6312
Fax: (800) 318-6312
www.flyball.org

Therapy Dogs, Inc.
P.O. Box 5868
Cheyenne, WY 82003
Telephone: (877) 843-7364 or
(307) 432-0272
E-mail: therdog@sisna.com
www.therapydogs.com

Therapy Dogs International
88 Bartley Road
Flanders, NJ 07836
Telephone: (973) 252-9800
Fax: (973) 252-7171
E-mail: tdi@gti.net
www.tdi-dog.org

United Kennel Club (UKC)
100 E. Kilgore Road
Kalamazoo, MI 49002-5584
Telephone: (269) 343-9020
Fax: (269) 343-7037
E-mail: pbickell@ukcdogs.com
www.ukcdogs.com

**United States Dog Agility Association
(USDAA)**
P.O. Box 850955
Richardson, TX 75085-0955
Telephone: (972) 487-2200
Fax: (972) 272-4404
E-mail: info@usdaa.com
www.usdaa.com

**World Canine Freestyle
Organization, Inc.**
P.O. Box 350122
Brooklyn, NY 11235-2525
Telephone: (718) 332-8336
Fax: (718) 646-2686
E-mail: wcfodogs@aol.com
www.worldcaninefreestyle.org

NATIONAL BREED CLUBS

Affenpinscher Club of America
Secretary: Jo Acton
E-mail: jogahri@aol.com
www.affenpinscher.org

**American Brussels
Griffon Association**
Secretary: Linda Vance
E-mail: fistfaces@aol.com
www.brussels-griffon.info

**American Cavalier King Charles
Spaniel Club, Inc.**
Secretary: David Kirkland
E-mail: rokirk@alltel.net
www.ackcsc.org

American Chinese Crested Club
Secretary: Patricia Bickerstaffe
E-mail: CamelotChinese
Crested@cox.net
www.crestedclub.org

American Maltese Association
Secretary: Barbara Miener
www.americanmaltese.org

American Pomeranian Club, Inc.
Secretary: Cindy Boulware
E-mail: contact@American
PomeranianClub.org
www.americanpomeranianclub.org

American Shih Tzu Club
Secretary: Bonnie Prato
E-mail: HANASHIHTZU@
compuserve.com
www.shihtzu.org

American Toy Fox Terrier Club
  Secretary: Margi Hill
  E-mail: secretary@atftc.com
  www.atftc.com

Chihuahua Club of America, Inc.
  Secretary: Tanya Delaney
  E-mail: Elfin987@aol.com
  www.chihuahuaclub
     ofamerica.com

English Toy Spaniel Club of America
  Secretary: Susan Jackson
  www.etsca.org

Havanese Club of America
  Secretary: Jane Ruthford
  E-mail: secy@havanese.org
  www.havanese.org

Italian Greyhound Club of America
  Secretary: Lynette Coyner
  E-mail: CharisIGs@aol.com
  www.italiangreyhound.org

Japanese Chin Club of America
  Secretary: Betty Stovall
  E-mail: bstovall@japanesechin.org
  www.dogshowgallery.com

**Miniature Pinscher Club
of America, Inc.**
  Secretary: Christine Filler
  E-mail: MPCASecretary@minpin.org
  www.minpin.org

Papillon Club of America, Inc.
  Secretary: Carol Morris
  E-mail: information@
     papillonclub.org
  www.papillonclub.org

Pekingese Club of America, Inc.
  Secretary: Leonie Schultz
  E-mail: Edenhill7@aol.com
  www.pekingeseclub.org

Pug Dog Club of America
  Secretary: Polly Lamarine
  E-mail: lamarine@sbcglobal.net
  www.pugs.org

Silky Terrier Club of America
  Secretary: Louise Rosewell
  E-mail: STCA@yahoo.com
  www.silkyterrierclubofamerica.org

Yorkshire Terrier Club of America, Inc.
  Secretary: La Donna Reno
  E-mail: ytca_sec@ytca.org
  www.ytca.org

INTERNET RESOURCES

AboutDogsOnline.com
  (http://www.aboutdogsonline.com)
  This website offers an array of
  information on topics like dog
  adoption, animal shelters, training,
  and health.

I Love Dogs.com
(http://www.i-love-dogs.com)
An extensive directory of dog-related
websites, I Love Dogs.com features
links to dog associations and clubs,
newsletters, memorials, breeders, and
many other informative sites.

PUBLICATIONS

AKC Family Dog
American Kennel Club
260 Madison Avenue
New York, NY 10016
Telephone: (800) 490-5675
E-mail: familydog@akc.org
www.akc.org/pubs/familydog

AKC Gazette
American Kennel Club
260 Madison Avenue
New York, NY 10016
Telephone: (800) 533-7323
E-mail: gazette@akc.org
www.akc.org/pubs/gazette

Dog & Kennel
Pet Publishing, Inc.
7-L Dundas Circle
Greensboro, NC 27407
Telephone: (336) 292-4047
Fax: (336) 292-4272
E-mail: info@petpublishing.com
www.dogandkennel.com

Dog Fancy
P.O. Box 6050
Mission Viejo, CA 92690-6050
Telephone: (800) 365-4421
E-mail: barkback@dogfancy.com
www.dogfancy.com

Dog World
P.O. Box 6050
Mission Viejo, CA 92690-6050
Telephone: (800) 365-4421
E-mail: dogworld@
        dogworldmag.com
www.dogworld.com

Dogs Monthly
Ascot House
High Street, Ascot,
Berkshire SL5 7JG
United Kingdom
Telephone: 0870 730 8433
Fax: 0870 730 8431
E-mail: acc@rtc-mail.org.uk
www.corsini.co.uk/dogsmonthly

ANIMAL WELFARE GROUPS AND RESCUE ORGANIZATIONS

American Humane Association (AHA)
63 Inverness Drive East
Englewood, CO 80112
Telephone: (800) 227-4645
Fax: (303) 792-5333
www.americanhumane.org

American Society for the Prevention of Cruelty to Animals (ASPCA)
424 E. 92nd Street
New York, NY 10128-6804

(continued) ASPCA
Telephone: (212) 876-7700
www.aspca.org

The Humane Society of the United States (HSUS)
2100 L Street, NW
Washington DC 20037
Telephone: (202) 452-1100
www.hsus.org

VETERINARY RESOURCES

Academy of Veterinary Homeopathy (AVH)
P.O. Box 9280
Wilmington, DE 19809
Telephone: 866-652-1590
Fax: 866-652-1590
E-mail: office@TheAVH.org
www.theavh.org

American Academy of Veterinary Acupuncture (AAVA)
66 Morris Avenue, Suite 2A
Springfield, NJ 07081
Telephone: (973) 379-1100
Fax: (973) 379-6507
E-mail: office@aava.org
www.aava.org

American Animal Hospital Association (AAHA)
P.O. Box 150899
Denver, CO 80215-0899
Telephone: (303) 986-2800
Fax: (303) 986-1700
E-mail: info@aahanet.org
www.aahanet.org/Index.cfm

American Holistic Veterinary Medical Association (AHVMA)
2218 Old Emmorton Road
Bel Air, MD 21015
Telephone: (410) 569-0795
Fax: (410) 569-2346
E-mail: office@ahvma.org
www.ahvma.org

American Veterinary Medical Association (AVMA)
1931 North Meacham Rd-Suite 100
Schaumburg, IL 60173
Telephone: (847) 925-8070
Fax: (847) 925-1329
E-mail: avmainfo@avma.org
www.avma.org

Index

PHOTO CREDITS

Carole Archer, 23, 31, 44, 55, 74, 99, 101, 102, 103, 112
Paulette Braun, 118
Isabelle Francais, 8, 12, 14, 16, 19, 21, 24, 28, 34, 38, 40, 41, 46, 48, 50, 52, 59,
    64, 69, 72, 77, 83, 86, 88, 90, 93, 95, 98, 106, 109, 120, 128, 130
Lara Stern, 122
Judith E. Strom, 117
Cándida M. Tómassini, 9